Call Me Coach

Alaska's Greatest Wrestling Stories

Steve Wolfe

Since 1978

PO Box 221974 Anchorage, Alaska 99522-1974

ISBN 1-59433-029-8

Library of Congress Catalog Card Number: 2005902413

Manufactured in the United States of America.

Dedication

To all the Homer High School Wrestlers from 1964 to today.

Acknowledgements

To my Dad, Ed Wolfe, a much better writer than I; he has always inspired me to do my best; and to my wife of 32 years, Nina, who constantly makes me happy.

Foreword
by Larry Kaniut

When I began coaching wrestling in Anchorage in the 1960s, the mention of Homer wrestlers like Covalt, Rozak, Turkington, Poindexter, Nixon, and Anderson struck terror among the state's wrestling community. They were smooth and they were good. Thirty-two years later, Coach Steve Wolfe asked me to look at his manuscript about Homer wrestling and, recently, to write a foreword.

My initial thought was he might sell 100 copies to family, friends, and mat rats! After all, how much demand is there for a book about a small town wrestling team—especially an Alaska one?

And how does Steve dispel the myriad myths and misinformation about wrestling? For instance, in the 1980s I overheard a collegiate wrestling coach state, "Unless a kid is in a bar eating beer glasses or I have to bail him out of jail, he ain't a wrestler."

Fortunately not all coaches are Neanderthals. Steve Wolfe is one of the good guys. He coaches character development, athleticism, and playing within the rules-on the mat and off. He has proven that good guys DO finish first.

And taking it a step further, as I settled into the book, I realized that it is not a wrestling book per se. Rather it is a book about a journey—not any journey but that of Steve and Nina and their move from Idaho to Alaska. Call Me Coach encompasses small town Alaska-atmosphere, working (commercial fishing, logging, farming-ranching), politics, local events, community camaraderie, and problems.

Even though the story line chronicles Steve's experiences while focusing on his coaching, his journey parallels ours. We all travel from cradle to grave. Although we follow different paths, we engage in most of the same activities. Steve follows his dreams, determined to achieve positive results; his love of students and athletes stands out as he fights to put them first; his principles prevail as he demonstrates proper protocol; he shares anecdotes regarding teaching colleagues; and he proudly proclaims his pride in his family.

I loved Steve's humor. I saw myself in many chapters. And I think you will too. I hated to turn the last page. If you like facing challenges and learning about life on the Last Frontier, you'll like this book.

Larry Kaniut

Preface and Disclaimer

In reality I moved to Alaska twice in my life, once as a boy and once as a schoolteacher. For brevity and to make the story a little easier to write, I combined many of the incidents of both arrivals into one. Because I chose this manner of presenting the material, many of these stories had to be edited from their actuality. However, these incidents are mostly true, but some did not happen in Homer and some did not happen to me. For example, the story of the bear in Chapter 13 did not happen to me, but it did happen to my Dad on his homestead in Alaska.

My wife claims I couldn't write anything about my life without it being fiction because, as she says, I remember things so much different than they really were. Therefore I have changed nearly all the names except some of my very close friends and family so that my memory and others might not disagree as much as they might.

The title of the book comes from the fact that I always insisted the wrestlers call me Mr. Wolfe, Sir, or Coach. Most called me Coach. I hoped those were terms of respect. I have always tried not to sulley, by my actions, the title of Coach. I'm not sure of the results of my insistance, but I do know that students and wrestlers from that first class, adults now in their 40s, still call me Coach.

Chapter 1

Like a flash of lightning the incandescent beauty of the scene below embraced me. With intangible fingers its tenacious loveliness reached in and clutched my very soul. I could breathe in only short little breaths, but breathing wasn't important. The beauty of this place was everything.

I was standing on Baycrest Hill overlooking Homer, Alaska. The town of Homer was a few buildings, haphazardly but somehow artistically nestled in the landscape below. To the left was the jewel-like blue of Kachemak Bay, to the right was wild, deep ocean blue of Cook Inlet. Separating the forces of the inlet and the bay was a thin sandbar, "the Spit," jutting six miles straight out into the water wilderness. One instantly felt affection for this dike-like bead of sand which stands its ground amid so much of the forces of nature.

Across Kachemak Bay, rugged snowcapped mountains jutted into the sky like bare teeth. Between them flowed the milky green of glaciers winding their way down, but never quite meeting the ocean. On this side of the bay all was green.

To see a lush green field was always beautiful to me, but here was green beyond my imagination. Everything was green, whether it was the bright green of the constantly fluttering little leaves on the birch trees or the deep green of Sitka spruce. And the grass, not waist-high lush grass, but six-foot-high lush grass, waving in the breeze like laughter. Another plant I had to inspect closely to see what it was. Fireweed. I'd seen fireweed before in my home state of Idaho. It was a straggling small plant which grew proficiently the year after a forest fire. But I'd never seen fireweed that grew like bamboo. Its stalk was the size of my finger, growing straight up the height of the grass. Long thin leaves protruded pedal-like the entire distance up the stalk. It had a little cluster of pink blooms at the top, tinging the native field with pinkish red.

If I'd tried I would have had no capacity to imagine this heavenly place. I wished I was a poet. Nothing less than poetry described Homer. I was in love. How did I get so lucky to get a teaching and coaching position in the most beautiful place in the universe?

I thought back to a time just seven months earlier when I received a call from the administrative building of the college I was attending.

"Steve, this is Lane Zeller. I have an interview for you with a Mr. Robbins. He's looking for a head wrestling coach."

"Great," I said. "When do I meet him?"

"Well, he's only in town today. Can you come up in the next hour?"

"Sure." At least I didn't have to travel for this interview. "Which school district is he from?"

"He's from Alaska, Steve. See you in a few minutes," and Lane hung up.

"Alaska. Now what has Lane got me into?"

Lane was the wrestler who in the off-season used to go down to a local bar and get in some row with a bunch of Marines or cowboys or professional football players, then call up his teammates and ask for help. Most of us didn't hang out at bars, but we were all for helping out a teammate. So we'd rush to his aid and about the time the fight really got going, we'd look around and Lane was gone, while we were looking up at 20 ugly and angry Marines. Now he had set me up with a recruiter from Alaska.

With a what-am-I-getting-into-now attitude I put on my best clothes and met the appointment at the administration building. I was introduced to a Mr. Robbins who soon put me at ease. He was kind of a short, dumpy fellow, but was full of energy. He had an easy, affable nature that made me feel comfortable at once. But what made me instantly like him was his obvious love of wrestling. He just beamed when the subject came up.

"How good a wrestler are you?" was his first question.

That was a hard one to answer. I thought I was the best in the world, and it was just a matter of luck I had only an 8-8 win-loss record, but for an interview I had to be modest. "Pretty darn good," I said. "I'm a varsity wrestler here. Last year we took fourth in nationals and this year we'll do better. Coach says I know more moves than any other wrestler he knows."

"That's great, that's great," Mr. Robbins said, beaming his enthusiasm. I wondered what Lane had told him about me. "We need a real coach in Homer, where I'm the principal." Then he proceeded to tell about this small Alaska town that had a great tradition in wrestling, and how he'd coached the kids and they had great desire, but he knew so little about wrestling that he couldn't teach them well and he needed a good coach, and I was it.

He talked in the run-on sentences of a car salesman, so I didn't need to say much. He'd already sold himself on me and knew I'd take the job. "What's your major?"

"P.E."

"Minor?"

"Spanish."

"What I really need is a history teacher. Would you like to teach history?" he asked.

"Well, my first two years I majored in archaeology, so I have a pretty good background in history," I explained. I was kind of getting caught up in his enthusiasm.

"Wonderful, wonderful," Mr. Robbins was practically running around the room, all the time rubbing his hands in glee. "You see," he said, "I can assign any certified teacher to any need I may have. I need a history teacher and you are certified?"

"I'm doing my student teaching now and will have my certification at the end of the semester."

He was now jumping up and down in one spot. "Oh, this is perfect, perfect. I want you to make Homer the best wrestling team in Alaska. Steve, I can call you Steve, can't I? Here's my handshake. That's the way we do business in Alaska. Now here's a contract. No hurry to sign it. Send it in when you can fill in the date of teacher certification and you're hired. I just can't wait for you to come to Homer."

I took that as a cue to exit and left, still a bit dazed. I always dreamed of being wanted, but somehow this bordered on being railroaded. I headed down the hallway to see Lane and ask him if this was a real interview, but Lane was not in his office; his secretary assured me that Mr. Robbins was a principal from Alaska. I looked and it was a real contract in my hand. Nearly $19,000. That was almost twice what I hoped to be paid for teaching. But in Alaska? I could just imagine wrestling in a big igloo. Wrestling mats get pretty hard in the cold don't they? I wasn't sure I'd ever wrestled on a cold one.

I went home, still a little dazed, put the contract with our other important papers and promptly forgot it. I continued my studies, my wrestling and looking at other career opportunities.

Graduation finally came. Even having my coach's best recommendation, it became obvious that the best jobs open to me would be a few junior high and assistant coaching jobs for less than $9,000 per year. Somehow I wanted to go to some little place and carve out a wrestling dynasty. It looked like my only opportunity to do that would be in Alaska. There probably was no littler place than Homer, Alaska. At least the pay wasn't bad. I was still a little concerned about wrestling in an igloo, but I signed the Alaska contract and sent it off.

A few weeks later I received a note from Mr. Loosely, who informed me that Mr. Robbins was no longer the principal, but the contract I had signed would be honored. Later I found out that Mr. Robbins was a wonderfully enthusiastic man, but he was also a crook. He had a background of hoodwinking people in the many areas he'd lived. He had promised several more positions to people than were open. I was just able to slip in. When Mr. Robbins was fired, he went to the school when no one was there and took every TV, microwave, camera and other valuable item, and sold them at his moving sale. He sold every item for a goodly amount of money and left before anyone was the wiser. There are many an old TV, VCR and micro-wave still being used in Homer homes that have the old school num-bers engraved on them, a legacy to Mr. Robbins.

So here I was at the most heavenly place in the world, not sure I was welcome. I felt like a sinner who'd somehow slipped through the pearly gates just knowing that St. Peter would probably be toss-ing me out any minute. But I was here. There was even a house to stay in free for the winter. A bit of a story in itself.

Chapter 2

When I got the job in Alaska, the most excited person in the family was my dad. It seems he'd always wanted to live in Alaska, but the farm had kept him so busy he just never got around to moving. But now he had to help me move. So he loaded up his old farm truck with a refrigerator, stove, a washing machine and everything else he felt a young couple would need. Most of the stuff was used, but in working order. He insisted we drive it up to Alaska. He'd read everything about Alaska, so he knew you needed extra gas and spare tires to drive the 2,000 miles of gravel road through Canada and Alaska on the "Alcan Highway." So he loaded two 55-gallon barrels of gas on the truck and pumped them full of farm gas. He found six spare farm truck tires lying around and loaded them on. We didn't have much room for our stuff, but he declared us now ready for the Last Frontier. "Someday I'm gonna come up fishing," he said. "They say you can catch salmon the size of hogs an' halibut the size of horses."

You could tell Dad was excited. He had that same sparky gleam in his eye that always came out when he talked about fishing. I never shared his enthusiasm for fishing. I had done a lot of fishing and not much catching, but Dad was excited. We loaded up our few college belongings and headed for Alaska.

I doubt there is anything that prepares a person for the Alcan Highway. The Alcan was built during World War II to make it possible for military supplies to be brought overland to Alaska. The sea route was deemed somewhat unsafe after Pearl Harbor. No expense was spared. However expense didn't make a better highway; it just made it expensive. It was a "cost plus" job. The contractors got expenses plus a percentage of what they spent as payment for their work. The more they spent, the more they made. One old man in Canada told me he worked on the Alcan and was told to go out in the woods all day 'til quitting time. He spent most of his time playing cards with the other guys who had been sent out in the woods all day 'til quitting time.

I noticed right away that the road curved snake-like where it should have been straight as an arrow. Someone quite reliable (he owned a gas station along the Alcan) told me that the road was so curved to prevent military convoys from being strafed from the air and completely destroyed. However, when I'd turned from right to left and back for the two-thousandth time, I was convinced the contractor must have been curving the road to get more road and thus more money. There had to be some idiot to blame for all these curves.

During all seven days it took me to drive the old farm truck up that gravel road, I conserved those two 55-gallon barrels of gas for the endless stretches where one could get no gas. However, every 40 to 50 miles, along the whole 2,000-mile stretch, there was always at least one gas station. When I finished the trip I still had two full 55-gallon barrels of gas and six unused spare tires.

We pulled into Eagle River Campground near Anchorage to rest up for the last leg of the journey, and there I fell into a good piece of luck. I pulled into a camping spot right next to another old farm truck. As I was unpacking for the night, I noticed the other truck driver was trying to fix his flat bald tire. Being neighborly, I spoke.

"Howdy," I said, very articulately.

"Hi there young fella," he returned. "Just moving into Alaska?"

"Yep," I said even more articulately.

"Well, Alaska is a great place. I'm sorry to leave it, but sometimes things just work out that way. Where you going to?"

"Homer," I said.

"What a great coincidence," he yelled as he pounded me on the back. "That's where I'm from! You picked the best place in the world. This your wife and kids? Great looking kids. Tell me, why are you going to Homer?"

"I'm the new wrestling coach at the high school."

"I didn't even know they had wrestling at Homer. Well, it's a great school and a great place. You'll love it. My name is George Henry Mayne; everyone just calls me Henry. This is my wife Ann and our kids George, Henry, Ward, Rosey, Georgia and little Henrietta. We're headed for New York City. We've been up here 15 years and it's time to see civilization again."

I'd never been to New York City or Arkansas, but judging from what I'd seen so far these people belonged in Arkansas, not New York City. But I didn't say anything about that. "My name is Steve Wolfe, and this is my wife Nina and kids Ivan and Becky. Looks like you had a little tire trouble."

"That's right, sonny, there's 240 miles of gravel road between here and Homer, and I had four flat tires," he said as he shook his head. "I should be all right if I can get this dad-burned thing off the rim."

"Let me see if I can help." I got out all the tire tools Dad had insisted I needed to fix all the flats I'd get on those brand-new truck tires he had installed on our old International. Finally I was using them for something. As we worked, I noticed Henry's tires were the same size as mine. With six extra spares and my trip nearly done, I figured I needed at most two so I asked if Henry could use the other four.

"I sure could, Steve." He was real comfortable using my first name right off. "But I don't have much money to pay for them."

"Heck, I didn't want any money for them," I said. "You can have them, I don't need them and they're pretty good tires. You might as well get some use out of them."

"That's mighty grand of you, young fella. I'll tell you what. Since you're going to Homer you probably need a place to stay. I have a nice two-bedroom home you can stay in for the winter free of charge if you want. Sometimes it's hard to find a place to stay in Homer and this house is only seven miles out of town."

I was flabbergasted. That was the only thing I was worried about. I had no place to stay and no money to pay for any. I'd put myself through college with a little help from a wrestling scholarship, but college was done and so was the money. We'd come to Alaska on our last bit and it would be a long time 'til our first paycheck.

"Gee, Mr. Mayne" (I wasn't quite comfortable calling him Henry yet), we really do need a place to stay. If it isn't too much trouble, we'd be glad to stay the winter."

He clapped me on the back and hee-hawed while his ample belly jiggled. We finished fixing the tire and got the tires down out of my truck. He gave me a letter to Cal Jesse saying we had permission to stay in his place. Then he gave me detailed instructions how to get there. The instructions were so well-done and detailed that we would easily be able to find the house.

I never saw or heard from Henry Mayne again. He never wrote; never left an address. I wonder if he is still in New York, or has moved to Arkansas? He never came back to Homer that I know of, but just before he left he put his arm around me and said, "There's a lot of wonderful people in Homer and some not so wonderful, but remember this: Don't ever have any dealings with Schifty."

I was grateful for the use of his home at that time. Little did I know what a "two-bedroom" house meant in Homer, Alaska.

Chapter 3

After Nina and I spent at least an hour gazing at the beauty of this little jewel-by-the-sea, commenting on how utterly gorgeous a sight it was and taking pictures, we finally came back to earth and decided to find our home for the winter. Mr. Mayne's directions were explicit. We drove right to the place.

My first comment was, "Well, it doesn't look like much from the outside, but I'll bet it's cozy."

"What do you mean?" said Nina. "It's a shack." She was right. It was a terrible shack. Slabs were the exterior wall covering; the bark was peeling away from the weather-worn gray boards. The roof sagged and the frame tilted slightly to the northeast corner.

"Maybe it's better inside," I said with the enthusiasm that comes from abject despair. We entered the shaky porch and I noticed that the covered porch was tilted to the west. The door was un-locked, and there was plenty of light from several windows. The floor covering was tent canvas. Someone had been raising chick-ens inside or at least some chickens had found their way in. We had to dodge the chicken manure to check out the rest of the house which consisted of an addition at the east end and housed the two bedrooms Mr. Mayne had talked about. It was one room, big enough for two cots and separated into two sections by a cardboard partition. Clearly Mr. Mayne had exaggerated. Well, at least he didn't exaggerate about the furnishings. There was elec-tricity, as indicated by a refrigerator and several light bulbs hang-ing from the ceiling. There was a cook stove, heating stove, wash-ing machine in the corner and several other "convenience" items. Thanks to Dad, we had brought all of these items in the back of the truck, as well as enough other furnishings to get by. Mr. Mayne had told us to use anything that was there.

I was ready to get mad and start cussing Mr. Mayne, Alaska, our bad luck and even the chickens, when my wife said, "Well, it's sure not much, but we can make do."

"What?" I yelled. "This is a stinking hole!"

"Yes, it's a stinking hole, but it's free and we can fix it up to get us through the winter."

"You want to live in this stinking hole?"

"No, I don't want to live in this stinking hole, but I can, and we can get by. We don't have money for anything else," she matter-of-factly replied. "A 'stinking hole' is better than nothing." Nina was the expert on our finances and she had never given me a reason to doubt as to her ability. In our three-year marriage as struggling college students we had never bounced a check and our bills were always paid. She worked miracles with a few dollars. If she said we could afford nothing more, it was wise of me not to argue.

From that point on though, we had christened the place the "Stinking Hole." Years later our second daughter Nina Ellen, who was born that winter, would ask as we tucked her into bed, "Mommy, Daddy, was I born when we were living in the Stinking Hole?"

"Yes, dearie, yes. Now go to sleep," my wife would answer.

At that point the only thing to do was roll up my sleeves and get busy moving in. We began by ripping up the canvas floor covering to discover half- to one-inch cracks between the floor boards. The wind really came howling up through those cracks. I went outside to figure how to bank up around the house to prevent the wind coming in under the house. I'd just about got things figured out when an old Hudson (one of those big luxury machines of the early '50s that I thought were all in junk yards) screeched to a halt in front of the house. Out jumped a big man. In a full run he charged right up to me. Now, I was a national class wrestler, very few men scare me, and not that I was scared, but I was a might worried. Blood and mayhem were scrawled all over his face and this man was big. He was a head taller than me, his shoulders were half again as wide as mine and he outweighed me by 100 pounds.

"What the hell is going on here?" he yelled, two inches from my face. "You can't move in here."

"Henry Mayne said we could," I said, holding my calm as best I could.

"He did not!" Still yelling, "Henry said my buddy could live here!" Bellowing even louder.

"Are you Cal Jesse?" I asked.

"Yes, I am." He quieted down a bit with that question, clearly taken aback that I knew his name.

"Just a minute. I have a letter from Henry to you." I walked to the truck and rummaged in the glove box until I found the letter Mr. Mayne had given me at Eagle River Campground. I brought it back to Cal and he read it without ceremony.

"Yeah, that's from Henry all right, but I just don't understand it. He said my buddy could stay here this winter." He folded the letter, looked at Nina and the kids who had just come from the house to see what the commotion was. "Well, it's a big house," he said. "I guess it's big enough for all of you." I figured it wasn't a good time to argue with him.

Cal continued. "Well, I guess Henry told you that cook stove is mine and the other stove is mine and the refrigerator is mine and the washing machine and that old Jeep out back, that is mine."

"Well, no, Henry said they belonged to him and that we could use any of them if we wanted, but we brought our own stuff, so if they belong to you, I'll help you move them out," I replied diplomatically.

His attitude suddenly changed. He put his arm around me like we were old buddies. He asked where we were from, chatted about rodeoing in Idaho and introduced himself to Nina and the kids. He asked if we needed any help and, with his arm still around my shoulder, said, "I'll tell you what. There's a lot of good honest people in Homer and there's a lot of crooks, but you'll probably get by without any problems. But young man, don't ever have any dealings with Schifty."

I never did have any dealings with Schifty, but I did hear some things about Cal Jesse. The story was told one night by a neighbor who knew Cal in Montana. It was one of those cold Alaska nights that impels one to huddle around the stove and tell about ghosts or gossip or other equally true stories. This night the subject was Cal Jesse. He was supposed to have been a great rodeo cowboy in Montana. That was easy to believe because even now, 15 years after coming to Alaska, Cal was a frequent winner on the small rodeo circuit in Alaska. However, in Montana he occasionally spent time in jail for re-papering horses. Re-papering horses was the nefarious practice of buying registration and pedigree papers of dead horses, then buying a horse that fit the description on the papers and then selling horse and papers at a much inflated price because it was a "registered" horse. This practice was not only illegal, it was crooked. Cal finally had to leave Montana when he stole (or borrowed, depending on which way you looked at it) a registered quarterhorse stud to sire a few colts with his own mares. Cal, of course, had neglected to ask permission from the old man who owned the horse. Cal also hid the stud quite well. When the stud's owner heard by rumor that Cal had his stud, he sent the police who caught Cal trying to haul the stud out of the country. Somehow Cal escaped to Alaska. He was never extradited because his crimes were deemed too small. I don't know if the story was true, but Cal always did stay in Alaska.

In my dealings with Cal I found him to be a good neighbor. He'd drop anything he was doing to help you out if you asked. He expected you to do the same. One Saturday morning he woke the whole family at six o'clock because he needed another hand to help on a project he had going. He hadn't asked for help before that moment. Although he asked for help occasionally, I was grateful that

20

he never tried to move his buddy in with us that winter.

Cal helped me unload some heavy things from the truck and into the house. After he left, we went back to our business of clearing out the junk and trying to prepare the Stinking Hole to be lived in. Before either of us knew it, almost magically, a rather interesting character appeared in the middle of the room. He was a small man with gray whiskers all over his gaunt face. His beard had not grown long enough to be called a beard and was not short enough to be called stubble. It could only be described as whiskers. I always wondered how this little man was able to get such whiskers for I never saw him clean-shaven and he never grew a real beard, he always just had those gray whiskers.

The little man backed up to the stove as if to warm his backside, although there was no fire in the stove. He spit out his chaw. I didn't mind. We hadn't torn the canvas off that part of the floor yet. He said, "Well, it looks like ya got a lot of young'uns. My name is Hank Snyder. Did Henry Mayne tell you that this here stove is mine and that cook stove over there is mine and that wash machine is mine and that old Jeep out back is mine?"

"No, I said. "Cal Jesse was just here and he claimed all that stuff."

"Oh-oh," said Hank. "Well, did he claim that old car down the driveway and that axe out in that stump?"

"He didn't claim the axe," I said.

"Well, that's mine and those car doors out west..." When Hank got done there wasn't an item anywhere on the place that wasn't claimed. Of course, Henry Mayne claimed we could use any of the stuff he left, but we had everything we needed with our full truck. I just figured that Hank Snyder and Cal Jesse were putting in first claim on the salvage. I later found out that Henry, Hank and Cal borrowed from each other and seldom returned much so that none of them knew for sure what was whose.

Hank Snyder was a right friendly fellow. My son was fascinated with his hip boots. He crawled over to grab onto one and pulled on the floppy outer part. I'd never seen hip boots folded down and then back up again that way. The boots covered and protected from wetness up to his knee, not all the way up to his leg, as is more conventional. Later I ran across a lot of Alaskans who wore their hip boots in that manner, but before that day not only had I never seen hip boots worn like that, I had never seen hip boots worn very long out of the water. Hank strolled around in them like they were his everyday wear. And no wonder. He homesteaded 160 acres of the mushiest bog I'd ever seen. They called it "muskeg" around this area.

Hank told one story after another and then finally slipped away to "let us get at our work." Just before he left, he had to give us just one piece of advice. "Don't ever have any dealings with Schifty." As I later found out Henry Mayne, Hank Snyder and Cal Jesse were notorious in town for wheeling and dealing, but apparently all of them had been snookered one way or another by Schifty.

Chapter 4

We finally got moved in. Cal Jesse came over and helped us move in the big stuff and, of course, he needed me to help him cart off the big stuff Henry Mayne had left. Nina was able to make the place quite comfortable. We had running cold water and it wasn't that far to the outhouse. A local church gave us some Masonite to cover the floor so the cracks between the boards wouldn't be a major problem. The neighbors, what few we did have, were downright friendly.

Hank Snyder and his son Joe came over often and we listened to him talk. He'd proved up on his homestead land years ago by hand-seeding sweet peas on one of his muskegs. A "muskeg" is the local name for a peat bog. They are quite prevalent in some areas around Homer as well as in other places in Alaska. These bogs are so wet and boggy that sometimes even traveling across them on foot is not a possibility. However, the peas grew like the dickens; the homestead agent saw the abundant crop and signed him off as having planted his acreage with a crop. Not a pea was harvested though; the muskeg was too swampy to take any machinery on and that many peas were impossible to harvest by hand. Hank didn't especially want to make any money farming, he just wanted his log cabin and 160 acres.

At night Hank would come over and tell us story after story about his life, all of them so well-told you could almost believe them. One of his stories I particularly remember. It seems that he had been a Seabee during World War II. He'd been assigned to a unit in the South Sea Islands as a mechanic. One blistering hot summer day he and another fellow were working on a Sherman tank when Hank reached for the water jug and instead picked up a jug full of some odorless, colorless fluid used for some mysterious purpose in the operation of military tanks. Hank swigged about half a gallon before he realized it was not water. When he did realize what he had swallowed, he immediately drank some used oil to make him regurgitate, but it was too late. He passed out and didn't wake up until many days later in the hospital.

He spent months in the hospital; often the blood oozed out from his pores so bad that he "stuck to the bedsheets." Hank spent most of a half-hour describing the horrors he endured, the pain inflicted on his body by that odorless clear liquid and all the medication the doctors gave him to counter the effect. In the meantime, the war was over and because of his many ordeals he was one of the first mus-

Call Me Coach

tered out of the service. However, the permanent physical damage was extensive. Before the war he was six-foot, one-inch tall and weighed more than 200 pounds. His many ordeals had shrunk him to his present five-foot, two-inch, 130-pound frame. He had told that story so many times that he actually believed it.

The family grew quite fond of Hank and although we moved after that winter, we kept in contact. About two years after we moved to Alaska, Hank showed up on my doorstep with another man about his same size and said, "Mr. Wolfe, meet Mr. Wolfe." With that he introduced me to Bill Wolfe (no relation of mine) who had just bought Hank's homestead. Hank moved off to California, I believe. I wouldn't be surprised if he was writing science fiction stories. I'm sure he's telling them. If you ever see a science fiction writer in Hollywood and he's wearing hip boots and has gray whiskers, that's him.

24

Chapter 5

Mr. Loosely was a very dignified man. He looked like a lawyer, setting in the principal's chair with his navy blue pin-striped, three-piece suit with a red power tie. He was not particularly large, but impressive nevertheless. I found out later that he had been to law school, but had taken the school principal's job this year to earn enough to pay for his next year's law school. Mr. Loosely actually stayed several years before moving on. One was immediately impressed that this was an intelligent, fair man.

He stood and shook hands with me and invited me to sit. His office was in transition, but his desktop was neat as a pin. While he was principal I never saw it otherwise. After a moment's chitchat, he came right to the point. "Steve," he said, "I know you were hired to teach history, but there is no history job at the high school."

I was getting a mite worried about this time.

Mr. Loosely continued. "But I'm willing to honor our contract and we need a wrestling coach. A lot of people in town want wrestling and they want an experienced coach. I like your credentials in that area and you've come with good recommendations, but I don't have a high school position for you."

I was really worried now. My heart was pounding and my hands were sweating. A few more sentences like that and I'd see my whole life pass before me.

"However," said Mr. Loosely.

I never realized how relaxing a single word could be.

"I do have a sixth-grade math and science position open, and if you feel you can handle it, it's yours. We have a sixth-grade-though-high-school concept here, so you could still be the high school wrestling coach and I'd like you to also coach the junior high boys. Any problems with that?"

"No, I think I could do that okay," I said.

"I see you've had a number of science and chemistry classes while taking a P.E. major, so I feel comfortable with you teaching science. What about your math background?"

"I always loved math. I took several upper division math classes in college, just because I enjoyed studying it. Sixth-grade math, I can do that." About now the sweat just above my hairline was starting to evaporate as I realized that I had not come all the way to Alaska without a job.

"Welcome aboard. Mrs. Maite, our secretary, will guide you to your room and you can get started planning." He stood, smiled and shook my hand. The first day of school had started. I was in the door, I had a job, now I had to do something with it or I'd be out the door.

Mrs. Maite gave me a building plan and I made my way to my room. There wasn't enough room for all the students in the main building, so my classroom was a self-contained building set away from the main building. It was set up like a circus tent, looked like a circus tent and was removed like a tent when not needed. Homer was growing, and this portable would probably be needed for a long time.

The inside of my portable was interesting. Obviously the previous class had painted murals on the walls. But the workers who had disassembled and reassembled it had not considered that fact in their work. It took a few minutes of staring when I first entered the room to figure out where that half of man was and why the zebra legs went up and where they should be. After a minute I just ignored it. I better let someone smart figure that out. Later in the year several of the artistically talented students in my classes painted their own murals. This made me much happier; it was mentally fatiguing trying to figure out how the old murals went together. Every time I looked at one of the walls I couldn't help but try to put them back together the way they should be.

The first two days of school are for teachers to get ready for the year. No kids, just teachers. But in reality there is only one day because the principal, no matter who, finds some way to take up an entire day with workshops and meetings that are a repeat of the year before and very little gets done. Being optimistic and a little slow, after 20 years of teaching I learned that. But that year I was naive and still felt I had two days to get ready for classes. So when the several teachers came by to chat, I was most accommodating and got to know several of them. There were some real characters in this school.

Chapter 6

Louise McDowell was an English and home economics teacher. She dropped by first. She wore a nice plaid skirt and sweater with wool socks and hiking boots. It seemed a strange combination, but already I'd seen stranger dress in Alaska. She liked to talk (I noticed a lot of people in Alaska liked to talk). Louise talked in "cannon time," like the old-fashioned cannon where you shot off everything and then had to reload. She would talk a blue streak and then suddenly get quiet as if to let you talk. But after she reloaded and began talking again, she took up where she left off as if you had said nothing.

She was from California and must have been one of the original members of Greenpeace and every other environmental protection society and agency. She jumped immediately on her band wagon about saving the environment and why she had come to Alaska where the air and water were still pure, how she loved wild animals and wanted to protect their habitat.

I got along quite well with her. I grew up on a farm and after I saw the harmony that existed on a farm between man, animals and plants, I was of the feeling that men should be good stewards of the earth. She, however, was much more militant that I ever thought of being. The old-timers in Homer all said that wolves had never lived on the Kenai Peninsula in memory or legend. Even the Indians said so. The winter after Louise came to Homer, a pack suddenly materialized. Years later it was discovered that a group of environmentalists had relocated some to the area, to protect them from trapping in other areas. The wolves were protected in Homer but the moose population was devastated in one season. Louise was reported to be part of that group (the environmentalists, not the moose).

We became relatively good friends. She was sometimes hard about the environmental issues (save the whales, the trees, the ducks and all other creatures and plants), but was good-natured when we teased her about her apricot-and-spinach sandwiches and tofu-prune pizza. She came up with some very strange lunch combinations.

Halloween that year she and her husband, Bob, invited us over for dinner. It is always nice for a young couple to be invited out for dinner. We got a babysitter and went over to a nice candlelight dinner. Knowing that they were vegetarians made me a bit apprehensive, but Nina was game so we said what the heck, it wasn't quite as good as trick-or-treating, but you only live once.

The spinach lasagna was downright good. At first I backed off from the chickweed salad (I'd pulled too many of those out of my garden as just weeds in my youth), but if you put enough dressing on it, it tastes like the dressing. So I was feeling fairly satisfied when they brought in this humongous pumpkin pie. It smelled delicious. It was the biggest, thickest pie I'd ever seen. I didn't know they made 20-inch pie pans and it must've been two inches thick, counting the crust. You could see pride written all over their faces. Bob and Louise had pooled their talents on the masterpiece. They began to explain:

"We feel that waste is a terrible thing," Bob said.

"So we used the entire pumpkin," added Louise.

"And," said Bob, "we used natural olive oil and whole wheat on the crust." They beamed at each other and cut generous slices for each of us.

I'd never had a slice of pumpkin pie that big in my life. It sat on the plate looking like a large row boat. Pumpkin pie was my favorite and I'd often wanted a chance to eat a whole pie. Here was my chance in just one slice, and it smelled absolutely divine.

I cut my first bite. Nina always says my bites are too big for polite company, and this was one in the category of big for sure. My tongue was quivering in anticipation and then I put the whole bite in my mouth ... it was the most awful thing I'd ever eaten. It tasted like some garbage cans smell. My throat tightened up, refusing to swallow the offensive mass. I was forced to chew it over and over, tasting it again and again. I finally forced myself to swallow in desperation and control my stomach which was rebelling.

"How is it?" Louise asked, leaning forward with the anxious look that just knows you are pleased.

"I've never had any pumpkin pie quite like it," I said. "How did you say you made it?" I continued the conversation just to delay having to take another bite. Eventually I had to choke the entire row boat down. I think I would have rather eaten 10,000 Russian Army socks. Somehow, through superhuman effort, I got the whole piece down and kept it down. Nina ate a few bites and then protested that she was too full, as only women have the right to do. Louise and Bob each ate a healthy piece and even seemed to enjoy it.

Although I grew up on a farm, my mother always made pumpkin pie with canned pumpkin. I had to buy a pumpkin some years later (when they no longer nauseated me) just to find out what I ate. When you open up a pumpkin, on the inside are pumpkin seeds in some slimy stringy matter that can remind you only of the intestines of a large rodent. I learned through sad experience you don't use that stuff for the pie. Unless you like the taste of an old garbage can.

The thing that most imprinted Louise and her husband Bob in my mind is what they did to Bill Wolfe's place.

Old Bill Wolfe had bought Hank Snyder's place which was a large muskeg. Old Bill was a hard worker. He took his shovel and ditched by hand 20 acres of the muskeg. He divided every 50-by-50 foot plot of all 20 acres with a narrow hand-dug ditch about five feet deep. The peat bog of a muskeg is so thick that it took a ditch that deep to drain water away from the spongy ground. As far as I know, no one had ever undertaken such a task and to this day no one has again. Bill sloped all the ditches just so that the water drained off to the local creek. The muskeg drained rapidly. With a hand rototiller Bill tilled up the dried-out soil and planted strawberries over the entire 20 acres. The terrific change in soil climate killed all the weeds and the peat bog was the most fertile soil anywhere. The strawberries thrived. Some of his strawberries grew to be the size of apples and Bill cared for them from sun-up to sun-down (which is a long time in the Alaska summer) like they were his children.

Bill sold bushels every week all summer long to the local Alaska Wild Berry Products. He also let people come and pick-for-pay. There were enough strawberries for everyone in the whole area. Bill was proud as punch of his project and rightfully so. However, Bill was getting old. His wife had died and he figured he needed to sell out and retire. He put his 160 acres up for sale and to my surprise it was Bob and Louise who bought it. I thought at first that this place would be perfect for these back-to-nature people, but to my horror Bob and Louise immediately built a dam in the creek and flooded the entire 20 acres of strawberries to make a duck and geese refuge. It tore my heart out to see all those strawberries floating to the top of their man-made lake. I'm not sure that any ducks ever landed on that lake, but if they did, I'm sure they could have had all the strawberries they wanted.

Old Bill Wolfe must have been devastated when his strawberry plants he worked so hard for were drowned out, but he seemed to take it well. A few years later he died, Bob and Louise moved back to California, the dam broke and the lake drained. The water had eroded the ditches so that they had filled in and now this 20 acres is a muskeg again as it had been for thousands of years.

Chapter 7

Two things immediately came to my attention about wrestling at Homer High School. First, the boys in wrestling were starved for good coaching. Several wrestlers had some talent and wanted to be good, but the program was young and had been somewhat neglected the past several years. They had previously not had a coach with any real experience.

Second, another new teacher also had an interest in wrestling. He was Al Poindexter, a young man just out of college, like myself. He was the new P.E. teacher and had wrestled in high school. I met him the first day of school and liked him instantly. He was average-sized, a nice-looking young man, with no conspicuous physical characteristics except bright red hair. He could have borrowed the hair from Howdy Doody it was so brilliant red. He rarely smiled, and came across as a very serious and dedicated person. As we talked it was obvious that he had a lot of insights into how to make the wrestling team better. We had an unspoken agreement that together we were going to make Homer the wrestling dynasty of Alaska.

As I worked with Al through the years I found him to be a genius as a conditioning coach. He knew instinctively when the team needed to be pushed, when they needed slack time, how to get the team in peak condition at post-season tournament time and what and how much exercise was needed to achieve these goals. He also kept to the forefront of every new conditioning and training development. I learned never to question him on matters of conditioning; he was always right. He in turn never questioned me on the technical side of wrestling, deferring to my experience. We developed a team relationship that was enjoyable through the years. Any success we experienced in Homer wrestling was his success as much as anyone's.

The wrestlers wanted to start practice the first day of school. I suggested that they turn out for football or cross-country running.

"There is no football and you want me to run cross-country?" said Clarence, our 240-pound heavyweight. Poindexter was coach of the cross-country running team, so I strongly suggested that everyone run cross-country. But I had to agree that perhaps cross-country wouldn't be best for Clarence and some of the others. So I set up a practice of calisthenics, soccer and football. They loved especially the football which always started out touch and ended tackle. I saw right away that these kids were tough. Most of them were farmers, ranchers and fishermen in the summer. They knew how to work and have fun doing it. I could see a solid core of a fine wrestling team. Coach Poindexter said the wrestlers were the hardest working members of the cross-country running team as well. It looked like a bright future for wrestling at Homer High.

Soon wrestling season was upon us and we rolled out the wrestling mat for the first time. It was only one-year-old and you could see the pride in the wrestlers' faces as it was unrolled for the first time. It had been a long time since I had seen a mat so small. It was barely legal. Horsehair mats had to be placed on the outside of it to have a border because the square 24-by-24-foot mat was the entire wrestling area. Those familiar with wrestling know how important the border is to wrestlers. The border is as important to the safety of the wrestlers as the ropes are to a boxer. A great possibility of injury exists for those who wrestle close to the edge of the mat if borders are insufficient.

Wrestling mats have gone through a process of rapid change. When I first started wrestling in the early '60s wrestling mats often consisted of several horsehair mats pushed together and covered with a vinyl mat cover. This arrangement had many problems. The last wrestlers in the competition often found themselves wrestling around the gaps that developed between the mats. Sometimes a referee couldn't tell if the boy on his back was truly pinned. One or both shoulders would sometimes be in the crack between mats. It was wonderful when the new Ensolite foam rubber mats came out. Not only were they uniform in thickness, but they were so soft that an egg dropped from 20 feet wouldn't break.

Until the previous year, Homer had wrestled on horsehair mats. Now they had an Ensolite mat, although it was a little bit small. The kids thought it was great however. I thought that it would do and it did for several years. It was our practice and game mat for the next five years, for both high school and junior high.

That old mat taught me a great deal. It taught me that human ability rises to the height of the challenge. When the wrestlers first got the little old square mat, it was 24-by-24, one-inch thick and it was heavy. It was divided into three sections and it took six to eight wrestlers to carry each section. About five years later we got a new mat. It was 1-$\frac{1}{4}$ inches thick, 30-by-30 feet and it was heavy. It was divided into three sections and it took six to eight wrestlers to carry each section. After we got it, four wrestlers seemed to be able to easily carry one section of the old mat.

Five years after that we got another new mat. It was 1-$\frac{1}{2}$ inches thick and 34-by-34 feet. It was cut into three sections and it was heavy. It took six to eight wrestlers to carry each section. We still used the other mats for practice and tournaments. Four wrestlers could carry each section of the 30-by-30 mat and two wrestlers could tote each section of the little mat. In fact one wrestler, Stan Gear, could toss one section of the small mat on his shoulder and pack it himself. The mats never really changed in weight, but the wrestlers' outlook about the task of carrying mats changed tremendously. I called it "the parable of the wrestling mats."

A wonderful invention held the sections of the mats together. Called mat tape, it was a clear stretchable tape that could be run along the edge of the sections of mat to hold them together. When I first came to Homer it was always in short supply. We reused it as much as we could. Each night after practice we had to untape the mats and put them away because by day our wrestling room was the lunch room. To save tape we rolled the used tape up on pop cans, pop bottles, anything we could to save the tape. By the end of the year the tape was so well-used it barely held the mats together.

I was told new tape was never a possibility. Money was short, so we made do. Being somewhat naive that year I believed that to be true. Then came a dual match with Kenai late in the season.

Kenai High School was, and had always been, Homer's rival. The schools were in the same school district and supposedly funded equally. However Kenai was closer to the central office of the school district by 80 miles and thus tended to be the showcase school. Sometimes that was hard to tolerate for us outlying schools, but it was the fact.

I noticed before the match this particular day that they used brand-new tape for the mats. It was hard for me to recognize it since I hadn't seen new tape for two months, but sure enough it was new. I thought it was nice that they saved new tape for our dual meet. It made me feel kind of special. Here we were being treated like the honored enemies we deserved to be — new mat tape and all.

The match ended and with horror I watched as the custodian ripped up the mat tape and started rolling the tape into a ball in preparation to throw it away. I ran out on the mat and yelled, "Stop, stop!! Can we have this tape?" I then called to my team to get some pop cans to roll up the rest of the tape. We took that salvaged tape back to Homer, just tickled pink that we had some almost-new mat tape.

Chapter 8

The first year of coaching was gratifying. The wrestlers came to practice hungry for knowledge about wrestling. They did their best to learn anything we taught them and they were willing to do anything we asked. They would have run 50 miles and swam across the bay and back each practice if we asked them to.

We had three weeks of practice before our first match, and we really worked through those three weeks. I could see the kids were ready. When kids want to learn, they learn fast and well. They were eager and they couldn't wait to try their newly learned skills. Coach Poindexter had them in great shape and each practice they reminded me of a string of thoroughbreds held back at the gate. They couldn't wait for that first starting whistle.

In our first match we met Palmer which had not lost to Homer in seven years. The Homer boys wrestled like they'd been well-coached and they easily beat Palmer. The JVs also won, which was a cause of great celebration for the entire team. The next day we met our real challenge, "The Wasilla Takedown Tourney."

"How much are you over, Mike?" I asked. That statement contained the five most feared words at a weigh-in.

"Four pounds" was Mike's reply.

"You have half an hour to make it. Can you do it?" I asked.

"I don't think so, Coach," answered Mike.

Wrestlers lose tremendous amounts of weight in a short period of time by sweating, etc., but four pounds in a half-hour was a bit much for a 98-pound high school boy to lose. This had been a rough trip for Mike. It was his fourth year wrestling at 98 pounds. He had weighed 85 pounds as a freshman, but as is natural, gained some weight in those high school years. He was now a solid 110 pounds in the off-season and cut down 12 pounds to be at a weight where he felt he could wrestle competitively in state competition. He had placed second at the state tournament the year before and the fact that his best friend Ross wrestled at 105 pounds, the next weight class up, motivated him to wrestle at 98 pounds.

On the trip up to the tournament, Mike was chewing on Starburst candies and spitting in a cup to lose weight for the weekend. I had occasionally seen wrestlers chew gum and spit to get rid of enough body fluid to lose a couple pounds, but Mike had it down to a science. He had learned that Starburst really made him salivate. He needed to lose four pounds before the match at Palmer. One the 250-mile road trip up to Palmer, Mike spit and filled his milkshake cup four times with the most awful multi-colored mucus ever made. The rest of the kids could hardly stand to be around Mike when he was chewing and spitting Starburst. Mike spit off his four pounds and accidentally helped the whole team, including coaches, lose weight. Of course he received a little help from me.

It was a typical road trip for wrestlers, one like I have taken many times since. All 13 of us were packed into a school van, shoulder to shoulder, much like sardines. You get used to the smell of 12 teenage boys who often don't wash very well, but of course it's not easy at first. Especially if any of them are fond of garlic or beans or some other noxious odoriferous weed.

The weather was clear, but there was lots of snow on the ground. In Alaska when the snow comes down so hard that the road crews can't keep up with it, they usually just plow part of the snow off and as cars drive by enough times the snow becomes hard-packed for a fairly smooth surface, although a bit slick. If you are lucky, they will sand these roads; this road was not sanded at all. After driving in Alaska one gets fairly adept at handling all sorts of problems on these slick roads. So when the car in front of me suddenly pulled over to the side and stopped, I knew just what to do. I hit the brakes, putting our van into a mini-slide. Then as I got down slow enough, I let up on the brakes and quickly steered around the stopped vehicle. However, the result-ant sideways jerk of the van caused Mike to lose control of his grip on his paper cup. It plopped to the floor of the van. Green, yellow, blue, red and purple mucus oozed across the entire floor.

Total chaos resulted in the van. Everyone's feet went up in the air to keep away from the multi-colored blob. At the same time every window came open with two or three wrestlers' heads out, spilling their cookies. In the same distress, I pulled over to the side of the road and joined Coach Poindexter and all the wrestlers (except Mike) hurling on the snowbank. None of us would go anywhere near the van until Mike had cleaned it up. Mike ruined a good towel wiping up the awful mess. Then we wouldn't let him throw the towel on the side of the road as litter, so he hung it on the back bumper of the van where it froze and stayed the rest of the trip. I'm sure no one ever used that towel again.

Mike made weight that day and won his Palmer match, but he couldn't restrain himself enough to keep the weight down for the next day. Mike was not the only wrestler who had that problem; two of my other wrestlers were overweight. Rather than a strong team, it looked like we might have only an average team. Three of our stron-gest wrestlers did not make weight.

"Tell the Torgustad brothers not to worry about making weight. We'll put in the JVs," I called out to our manager. "Mike, I'll forgive your debut weekend, but let's not let that happen again. Let's get down to weight and stay there."

Mike looked down, real disappointed in himself, and said, "okay, Coach."

With a red face, I made my way to the coaches meeting to make my substitutes. As years went along I learned that this happened to every coach occasionally, but at this first tournament I felt it had never happened to anyone in the history of the world of wrestling before this day. Making the changes turned out to be much less painful that I thought they would be however.

Wasilla High School was running a "takedown tournament." A takedown tournament is a little bit different from most tournaments in that wrestlers do all their wrestling in a standing position. When one wrestler is able to gain advantage over his opponent by taking him to the mat and gaining control over him, it is called a takedown. In any regular match the wrestling continues on the mat, but in a takedown tournament the referee stops the match and brings the wrestlers back to their feet to wrestle for another takedown. The winner is the wrestler with the most takedowns at the end of the match. It was a great way to start off the season. Wrestlers could concentrate on takedowns for the first part of the season and perfect a very important part of their wrestling.

It was exciting to be a coach at my first tournament. Coach Poindexter didn't seem as excited outwardly as I was, but I did notice his hands sweating. The kids were excited, not over-anxious, but excited to be there. The only damper on our excitement was three weight classes with JVs instead of varsity wrestlers.

I was particularly concerned with Roger Engles at 98 pounds. He was just a freshman and this was his first varsity experience. Mike easily trounced him in practice, so I was a little afraid how he might do in this tournament. He was also the first of our wrestlers to wrestle that day.

The time for Roger's match came. Coach Poindexter and I gave him our pep talk, slapped him on the back, rubbed his shoulders and gave him as much encouragement as we could. The team gathered around him and chanted, "go, go, go, go," which was a Homer custom. Before the last chant Roger was jumping up and down in place. On the last and loudest "GO," Roger leaped out of the middle of the group as if shot out of a cannon. He was in full sprinter speed when he hit the edge of the mat. For some reason the mat was not quite dry at our end and when Roger's feet hit the wet mat at top speed, both flew out from under him and up into the air. He made the most beautiful broad jump in wrestling history, flew 20 feet through the air, and landed rump first in front of his opponent. A hush fell over the crowd. Some were quiet because they had never seen anyone travel unaided through the air that far, others because they thought he might be hurt. But Roger jumped up physically unhurt, but very red-faced.

There is a lot of psychology to wrestling. I thought sure that Roger was so embarrassed that his experienced opponent had already won before the referee blew the whistle to start. However, Roger shook hands with his opponent, with the referee, and then wrestled like I've seldom seen a freshman wrestle.

It is satisfying to see any wrestler complete a "move," as a wrestling maneuver is called, a move you know you taught him. I wish all teachers had the opportunity to see their students display excellence in the field of knowledge they, the teacher, had the sole responsibility to teach. And to see it displayed publicly. It gives one a warm glowing feeling in the midsection.

My midsection glowed that day when I was at mat side with Roger. He nailed every opponent with takedown after takedown. Every takedown he executed was poetry in motion. Roger had no takedown scored against him and easily won the gold medal. I was extremely proud of Roger and met him at the mat center after his championship match and carried him off the mat (which is easy to do with a 98-pound wrestler). Not only was Roger successful, but the other two JV substitutes won their weight classes as well. We had seven champions and a couple of seconds and every wrestler placed in the top four.

You couldn't contain the kids when they announced Homer as the team champions. Those farm, ranch and fishermen kids whooped and hollered all night. It was the first trophy Homer had won in several years. They were excited and I was pleased, to say the least. They had learned everything we had taught them. Coach Poindexter's comment was that they were not in quite good-enough shape, but I knew they were the state championship team. Ah, the exuberance of youth and inexperience.

Roger was an excited kid, just a freshman and already a champion. Mike kept his promise, got down and stayed on weight the rest of the year. He was able to easily beat Roger, so Roger wrestled at JV the rest of the year and went undefeated. He was a boy destined for greatness in wrestling. The sad part of the story was that Roger, on a hunting trip later that spring, bent down to drink some water from one of those clear Alaska streams, and his pistol fell out of his holster, discharging and killing him. Roger was always a gentleman and well-liked at school. His death was a sad day for the entire school. To this day Homer High School gives out the Roger Engle Award to the wrestler who displays outstanding sportsmanship during the season.

36

Chapter 9

We had a great year that first year. As a team, we had a lot of fun. The fans related to us that Homer wrestlers could wrestle now. I was happy with the team's progress and enthusiasm. But when the regional tournament was finally wrestled, only two wrestlers got to advance to the state tournament — Mike Ferris and Ross Aydelott, wrestling in the 98-pound and 105-pound classes respectively. It is an interesting fact that there are often two wrestlers, from the same team, very near each other in weight, who do well together. Some say it is because they push each other in practice to excellence by wrestling with each other. That surely is part of the answer, but somehow I think there is a psychological factor that each inspires the other to greater success as he reaches greater success.

There are always moments of drama in a tournament and that first regional tournament was no exception. Most notable was the match between Allen Trammel from Homer versus Nelson Gorsuch from Kenai. Allen was a big strapping ranch boy. He wore cowboy boots, a big buckle, listened to country-western music and was as tough as the outdoors. As tough as Allen was, he could never beat Nelson Gorsuch who was a year older than he and one of the finest wrestlers in the state. Using the bulldog attitude he had learned from years of making cows do what they don't want to do, Allen jumped into every match with rugged determination to win this one. Kenai High School was Homer's traditional rival and somehow Allen ended up wrestling Nelson four times that year. The first time Nelson won by eight points, the second by six points, the third by four points and the week previously Allen had wrestled the match of his life to lose to the best wrestler in the state by only two points. Now they were at regionals, the winner of the match went to state and the loser stayed home.

I had never seen a wrestler warm up as much as Allen did for that match. Fifty push-ups, 50 sit-ups, 100 jumping jacks, running in place, jumping rope — Allen did it all. His square jaw was set with determination. This was going to be his match. He stepped on that mat knowing he would win. He shook hands with Nelson and when the referee blew the whistle, he attacked. Nelson countered, and Allen attacked again and again. Nelson countered and then counterattacked. Up, down, all around the mat these two wrestlers fought. It was one of those matches crowds love because of the action and excitement.

It was one of those matches that insure bald heads on coaches who are constantly pulling their hair out in frustration.

Several times it looked like Allen had Nelson figuratively on the ropes, then at the last moment Nelson would slip away and counter-attack. If every square foot of the mat wasn't wrestled on during that match, Louis Armstrong never sang the blues. When the final fur had flown, when the whistle was blown to end the match, Nelson Gorsuch had won by one point. It was such a great effort by both wrestlers that it was a shame that one had to be declared the loser. Allen, in my mind, was a winner, because he gave it every ounce of effort he had in that tough cowboy body.

Allen shook hands as he was supposed to in the match-ending ceremony, and then made his way to the edge of the mat. As he came off the mat he was breathing deep gasping breaths that he couldn't stop. He was obviously in distress as he gasped, only to be forced to gasp heavily and deeply again. Unable to stop the heavy breathing, he still felt as if he didn't have enough air and would gasp and breathe another long breath. It was a classic case of hyperventilation.

Hyperventilation in itself is not particularly dangerous. If untreated, the victim will eventually pass out and breathing will revert to normal. It is caused by a lack of carbon dioxide in the lungs. Carbon dioxide is used by the lungs to regulate breathing, and a lack of carbon dioxide causes the lungs to want to over-breathe. The victim feels as if he has no air, even though he really has too much air. And his deep gasping breaths are compounding the problem. This is a fairly common ailment in athletics; coaches and trainers are usually taught how to handle it. The trick is to increase the percentage of carbon dioxide in the lungs. A simple way to do this is to have the victim breathe in and out of a paper bag. The carbon dioxide that he breathes out will then be breathed back in and very rapidly the breathing will return to normal.

Allen obviously needed help, but I looked around in vain for anything like a paper bag. Allen had slumped to the side of the mat, gasping, and he obviously thought he was dying. I spied a towel and figured if I had him breathe in that he would eventually get enough carbon dioxide to help his breathing. Allen, however, did not understand what I was doing when I smothered his mouth and nose with a towel, and he reacted violently. He kicked, he fought, he jerked, turned and fought with every fiber of every muscle to get away from that towel. I in turn straddled Allen and with the tenacity of a bare-back bronc rider held the towel over his mouth and nose. The crowd roared; they thought another match had started and the coach was going for the pin. Allen fought harder at that moment than he'd ever fought in his life; he thought he was fighting for his life. I took the towel off his mouth when I saw he was all right, I left and went to the next match.

Later that day Allen came to me.

"Coach, I really thought you were trying to smother me. I thought I had lost the match and now the coach is trying to kill me. What did you do?"

I explained hyperventilation to him and what needed to be done to stop it.

"Well, it sure worked. After just a few breaths in that towel, I could breathe again. Thanks. For a few minutes I thought I was going to die. Then I knew I was going to die and the coach was killing me." Allen was just a little embarrassed. Kids don't always trust their coaches implicitly.

Nelson Gorsuch went on to win the state championship, got a full ride scholarship to college and eventually became a very successful wrestling coach. Allen Trammell wrestled his senior year, but his season was cut short by an injury. He eventually went on to college and that tough cowboy kid is now an executive with Microsoft. I'm not sure how he got from cows to computers.

The person my heart went out to this tournament was Russell Cotes. Russell was a mighty fine wrestler. It was hard not to like Russell. He had an easy-going attitude and a kind heart. He was such a good wrestler he'd been beat by only one wrestler the entire year. It looked like Russell would be going to state. In the semi-finals, Russell had to beat only one boy from Seward, a boy he'd beaten by large margins several times that year. Once he'd pinned him, which is the ultimate defeat. A pin is when one wrestler holds the shoulders of the other on the mat for two full seconds. In high school wrestling a pin is the object of the entire match.

Russell was warming up for his match with the Seward boy when he noticed his adversary wasn't warming up at all. Eventually Russell's Seward opponent came over to him and said, "Cotes, I know you're going to win, just don't pin me, okay?"

"I'm gonna do my best," Russell answered. But somehow the starch left Russell with that conversation. He walked out on the mat without his old vim and vigor, and yet at the same time he seemed confident. As it turned out, a little too confident. Russell went right for the takedown. He scored two points for the takedown and went right for the pin, and suddenly in his over-anxious state he pushed a little too hard and found himself on his back fighting to keep from being pinned. Russell fought off his back to stay alive in the match. The score was 5-2. The Seward boy had scored two points for a reversal and three points for a near-fall, putting him ahead in the score. He then went into a stall mode.

Now, stalling is illegal in wrestling. The referee is supposed to recognize it and penalize a wrestler who uses stalling as a tactic to win, but sometimes referees let it go by and this was one of those times. Russell was able to escape from him twice, getting one point each time. But the Seward boy would run off the mat each time Russell tried for another takedown. Time after time Russell tried for a takedown, and time after time the Seward wrestler stalled. No call from the referee. The match ended and Russell lost 5-4.

It is sad when the home-team boy loses any time. It is doubly sad when the home-team boy loses like that. Russell felt, I felt, indeed the whole world felt (with the exception of those who lived in Seward, Alaska) that Russell deserved to go to state. Russell recovered though. He came back the next year, went to state and placed fourth. Now he is a very successful painting contractor in Homer, and I hear he never believes anyone who says, "Just don't pin me."

Dave Moss was another boy I was just sure would go to state. He may have been the most gifted athlete I ever coached. He was a native Alaskan boy with the body of a miniature god. Every muscle was naturally well-defined and strong. Besides being strong, he had the speed and quickness of a hunting cat. In wrestling, usually a wrestler waits until he can touch his opponent before he shoots for a takedown, but I'd seen Dave shoot from 10 feet away and score the takedown. He would use everything he was taught to do and then he would make up wrestling moves at the instant and they would work. He was capable of the superhuman every match. No one had challenged him all year. He was undefeated and unscored on.

Dave had just one problem: before every match he would get violently ill. He would spend half an hour before the match sick over a trash can or a toilet, losing everything he had eaten all day. Somehow he would drag himself on the mat, wrestle great, and then run for the trash can after the match, where he would again be sick for a half-hour. Dave, his parents, and us coaches, all were very worried about him. He'd been to the doctor several times. The doctor could find nothing wrong. Dave seemed to be fine all week; he could endure the toughest practices, but every wrestling match he was sick. His parents decided finally to do something, so they all flew to a faith healer in the Phillippines. They promised to have Dave back for the regional tournament, but they didn't make it back in time and Dave was not able to qualify for state.

I was a young and inexperienced coach at the time and so did not recognize what was happening with Dave. Later I saw the same malady in other good athletes and I was able to help them deal with it. Everyone who approaches an athletic contest has a wonderful natural drug dumped in the bloodstream, called adrenaline. The side effects of the drug are sweating of the palms, frequent urination and sometimes an upset stomach. I've noticed that some people are able to put a great deal of adrenaline in their bloodstream. Because of this they often feel very sick before and sometimes after a contest. This illness does not impair their performance, it just makes them feel sick. Usually if the athlete understands what is going on he can more easily deal with the pre-contest illness. Those athletes who experience this adrenaline illness are often great athletes, able to do the seemingly impossible. To this day I wish I had understood this malady and helped Dave. He was truly one of the greatest wrestlers to wrestle in the great state of Alaska.

Chapter 10

For the wrestler and his coaches, the state tournament is the pinnacle of the season. After a long season of the most grueling work ever inflicted upon a high school kid, and tournaments of elimination, only the best wrestlers in the entire state meet to wrestle to see who is the best in the state. Only two people in each of the 12 weight classes from our region qualified for state. A coach only got to go if one of his wrestlers qualified, and this year we were taking two wrestlers: Mike Ferris, undefeated for the entire season, and Ross Aydelott, one weight class heavier. They were best friends. Ross also had won his weight class at regionals. Two of the 24 wrestlers from our region were from Homer. I had to feel good about that for the first year of coaching.

"Coach, how do I stop Allen's tight waist?" Mike asked me at one of those evening practices earlier in the season. Wrestling Allen from Kodiak was a real concern for Mike. Mike had finished third at state as a sophomore and second last year. Both times he'd lost to Allen from Kodiak.

"How does he do it?" I asked.

"Well, he reaches deep around the waist and grabs my hip bone. It squeezes my guts out and I can't seem to do anything with it. Everything I try he stops."

This was one of the many times that a wrestler had come to me after practice for help. Wrestling is a sport that is so complex, no one knows it all. But for every hold there is always a counter-hold or a counter-move. It is only after years of experience that one knows how to counter a move most effectively. I was a first-year coach, which gave me a lot more confidence than experience. I didn't know the answer, so I faked it with confidence, something all good first-year coaches can do.

"Mike, your best bet is a Hop-Out Granby. Here, let me show you. First you hop out your feet away from your opponent, then Granby roll back into him. If you work it right, you can get not only a reversal, but also a near-fall. Now let me talk you through it..." and I proceeded to instruct Mike in an effective counter.

I had a good college coach who used excellent teaching techniques to teach his wrestlers. He first explained and demonstrated the move he wanted us to learn. He then talked us through it by explaining how to do the move as we were doing it. Then he drilled us by having us do the move over and over until we had it perfected. I tried to follow his example with Mike and each of my wrestlers, trying to prepare them for every contingency in wrestling.

Mike never used the Granby against Allen, but we spent day after day of the week before state working on moves such as this to help prepare Mike and Ross for the tournament. Although the rest of the team had not qualified for state, most of them came in to practice just to wrestle with Ross and Mike to "keep them in shape." Most of the week we spent preparing Mike to beat two-time state champion, Allen from Kodiak.

When the weekend of the state tournament came, Coach Poindexter, Ross Aydelott, Mike Ferris and I made the 700-mile trip to Fairbanks for the High School Wrestling State Championship.

Coach Poindexter and I had been to a state championship as wrestlers, but this was the first for us as coaches. Ross and Mike had been there the previous two years; to them it was no big deal. When we got to the site school, they immediately found old buddies and were right at home. Coach Poindexter and I stood in the middle of the gym looking around and up at the decorations and posters like tourists in New York City. We were dazed. Mike had to yell at me three times to wake me up.

"Coach, Coach, Coach! Allen's not here!"

"What?" I said, jerking to attention. "What?"

"Coach, Allen is not here. He went up a weight class, then he got injured and he didn't make it to state." Mike couldn't contain his excitement.

"Is that right? Well, that's one person you don't have to worry about, but I hear there's a tough kid from southeast Alaska, a blind kid from Mt. Edgecombe. Then there is Spriggs from West Anchorage. His coach thinks he's going to go all the way. So maybe Allen is not here, but there's a lot of tough kids in this tournament." I had a tendency at the first of the year to tell the wrestlers how easy they had it with their opponents, to build their confidence, but that had backfired on me. It seemed that Homer kids did best against kids they thought were tough, and wrestled poorly against people they thought were easy. With this state tournament, I was adopting an everybody-is-tough policy.

"Yeah," said Mike. "I beat Spriggs last year, but he was tough. I never got to wrestle Noah from Mt. Edgecombe. He took third last year, but I didn't get to wrestle him. Allen beat him 1-0."

Now I was scared. Publicly I was quite confident that Mike could beat anyone, but if there was a kid who was beat only 1-0 by Allen, Mike might be in trouble. However, with the confidence that I didn't necessarily have, I said, "You've worked hard this year, Mike. These kids are tough, but you're tougher, right?"

"Right, Coach."

The seeding meeting went very well. The seeding meeting is a pre-tournament meeting of coaches and tournament officials to determine who is "seeded" first to fourth so the best wrestlers will not eliminate each other in the first rounds of competition. Wrestlers are seeded by their overall record and by how well they did the previous year at state. Seeding, however, often becomes complicated, especially when Wrestler A has beaten Wrestler B, Wrestler B has beaten Wrestler C and Wrestler C has beaten Wrestler A. At the same time all three have good win-loss records, and none of them placed in state the previous year.

Fighting for the seed positions is an art that coaches learn only after numerous seeding meeting battles and then only after the scars from these battles have healed. The seeding meetings are often tense times of political maneuvering that put Congress to shame and yet coaches who seem during the meeting ready to leap over the table at each other and duke it out, usually after the meeting are slapping each other on the back in hearty congratulations. In my many years of coaching in Alaska, I never saw coaches lose friendship for each other because of seeding meetings. They were always treated like an intense game of Monopoly. However, school and tournament officials never understood how much fun the coaches were having. These officials usually came out of a seeding meeting frowning, taking terse little steps, and muttering under their breath, "That was the worst meeting I've ever been to in my life. We've got to do something about seeding meetings." The coaches strolled out afterwards, laughing, slapping each other on the back and inviting each other out for a root beer. They had just had a great time.

This particular seeding meeting was a new experience for me. The old-time coaches were kind to us and after making us sweat, seeded our boys as they deserved. Even the most ruthless wrestling coach is usually pretty good about seeing that the wrestlers, all wrestlers, are not drastically hurt by their seedings. Mike was seeded first and Ross was seeded fourth, which was pretty fair to both of them.

And so the tournament began. Ross wrestled his heart out, placed fourth and had his high point in the tournament when in the semi-finals he wrestled the number one seed to a 6-6 tie, only to lose in overtime. Fourth was not bad, and he got a nice medal for his outstanding efforts that year.

Mike's tournament was a challenge. Although he was seeded first and should have had the easiest path to the championship, he ended up wrestling ever place winner in the tournament.

Mike ripped his first opponent 9-1. However, it was a close match until the last round. Mike was great at takedowns and easily took Keller, his opponent, down for two points. In the second round, Keller escaped for one point, but in the last round Mike reversed and then picked up two near-falls for two points each. The final score made it look as if this opponent was an easy match, but this young unseeded wrestler, Keller, went on in the tournament to take fourth.

Mike then had to wrestle the fourth-seeded wrestler. This was Spriggs, the wrestler from West Anchorage. West Anchorage as a team would go on to win the tournament. The coaches and their team smelled victory, and were all at the edge of the mat. Spriggs was undefeated this year, and his coach had been bragging that "no one will beat Spriggs this year." Spriggs was tough, but Mike, true to his form, got one takedown which was enough to win 2-0. Spriggs went on to place third in the tournament, but Mike was in the finals. Mike's opponent — Noah, the blind wrestler from Mt. Edgecombe.

"Coach, I've never wrestled a blind guy. What do I do? How can a blind guy even wrestle?"

"Mike, never underestimate a blind wrestler. I wrestled one in the Olympic trials and he was good. Let's go out on the mat. I want to show you something." We moved out onto the nearest mat.

"Now, Mike, I want you to get in referee's position on the bottom. Close your eyes. Now do an outside switch on me." Mike easily did an outside switch.

"Did you open your eyes?"

"No."

"How could you do it with your eyes closed?"

"I could feel where you were. I could almost see in my mind where you were."

"That's right," I said. "Now stand up. Keep your eyes closed and take my hands in this position." I showed him the hand position that wrestlers must use when wrestling with a sight-handicapped opponent. "Now, shoot a single leg." Mike easily completed a single-leg takedown.

"Did you open your eyes?"

"No," he replied.

"How were you able to do it?"

"I could see in my mind where your leg was."

"Keep your eyes closed. Don't touch hands." I stepped back and to the side.

"Now, shoot a single leg."

"I can't."

"Why?"

"I can't tell where you are."

"That's right. There is something about being able to touch his opponent that lets an experienced wrestler know where every part of his body is. Blind wrestlers can be great if they can only touch you. The rules say that you have to maintain contact with a sight-handicapped wrestler. You can't back off and shoot as you do to other wrestlers. You will be the one at a disadvantage, not Noah. To win this match you will have to wrestle your best, but you can do it. You're a winner; you'll find a way to win."

Nothing builds confidence like inexperience, at least with new coaches, and even with new coaches occasionally accidents happen and they say the right things.

That night one of the classic wrestling matches of Homer High history was wrestled. Mike Ferris, the Homer wrestler who had worked four years for this moment, for a chance to be state champion, versus Larry Noah, blind Indian boy from the small village of Mt. Edgecombe, both determined, each with their own talents, both seniors in the last wrestling match of their lives.

For a coach, being at the finals is an exhilarating experience. It's like the Academy Awards — the lights, the cameras flashing, 10,000 screaming fans (well, maybe more like 1,000). But it was exhilarating, and that was just for the coaches. I don't know how the wrestlers could handle it.

Most of the Alaska coaches at this tournament liked to show off how Alaskan they were. Some wore sweaters with a moose knitted on them. Some wore Carhartt coveralls and some even wore authentic Eskimo parkas. Gad, they must have been hot. Me, I wore what my college coach wore.

My college coach was an Oklahoma Indian who loved to dress up. He put on the best money could buy — sports jacket, tie, colored shirt, slacks and all. He always looked sharp. I was always proud he was my coach just because of the way he dressed. And I think that I wrestled a little harder because of that pride.

So here I was at my first state tournament as a coach, wearing a dark blue sports coat, dark blue slacks, bright yellow shirt, tie (tied in a full Windsor), all shining like only polyester can. I looked around and felt as much out of place as if I'd come dressed like I was to a livestock auction. But somehow the other coaches felt out of place too. I could see them looking at their Carhartts and wondering if they should have changed — maybe worn something else besides bunny boots.

I know that what I wore that night had some effect. In the years to come nearly every coach got all spiffed up for the state tournament finals. Some had washed their Carhartts, some had even put on three-piece suits and I think once someone even wore a tux. All were pretty well-dressed-up, except for Steele Jones. He always dressed "Alaskan."

After the announcements and introductions were made, wrestlers warmed up and primed. It was time for the 98-pound match.

The whistle blew and Noah immediately took advantage of the start and, using his great upper-body strength, pulled Mike into him and grabbed both of Mike's legs. A takedown seemed imminent. Mike hit a great whizzer counter, but was on the defensive. Noah kept Mike on the defensive, constantly pulling him in and trying for a takedown. Mike could only counter. If Mike would break away, the referee would immediately stop the match and start them again with the sight-handicapped touching start. Mike fought hard, Noah bulldoggedly, relentlessly pursued. Mike, in frustration and out of position, shot for a Fireman's Carry. Noah, taking advantage of Mike's position, countered and stuck Mike to his back. This gave Noah a two-point takedown and three near-fall points before Mike was able to struggle free and reverse Noah to gain two points. This meant that the score was 5-2 in Noah's favor at the end of the first round. I was sick with dread as the next round started.

In the folk-style wrestling of high school those years, only in the first round did the wrestlers face each other wrestling on their feet. In the second and third rounds, a coin toss determined which man was on his hands and knees on the bottom, and which man was in the so-called "advantage" position, or on top. The top wrestler was positioned a little behind the bottom wrestler, holding his waist and arm. It is called the"advantage" position because the top wrestler is theoretically closer to obtaining a pin. Most wrestlers, however, when they have the choice, choose bottom position because in practice it is easier to score points from the bottom position. They can do this with an escape, coming to neutral position (one point) or a reversal, coming to a position of advantage himself (two points).

Mike won the coin toss and chose advantage position, meaning that he would be in the bottom position during the last round. He swarmed over Noah, but the Mt. Edgecombe wrestler had been well-coached. He never got out of position. Mike pressed him, but found no opportunity to turn him to his back. Noah however took advantage of an opportunity and stood to escape. Mike quickly pulled him to the mat and just as quickly grasped Noah's right wrist with his right hand and put a half-nelson on with his left hand. Noah was a strong wrestler, but Mike took advantage of one instant to force him to his back and pick up three points for a near-fall before Noah wiggled free for an escape. That ended the second round. The score was 6-5 in favor of the Mt. Edgecombe boy.

Mike needed one point to tie, two points to win. This round he was on the bottom. In a brilliant flash of motion and with a mighty shrug of his shoulder, Mike stood up, turned and faced his opponent. The score now was tied. The referred stopped the match to again start the wrestlers in the appropriate "hand touch" position. Noah again went into his strategy of pull in the opponent and attack the legs. Frustration showing on his face, Mike fought off each shot, never able to counterattack. The third round ended; the wrestlers were tied 6-6.

In those days wrestlers who were tied wrestled an overtime match of three one-minute rounds after one-minute rests. During the minute rest, coaches had the opportunity to actually talk to the wrestler and coach him as to how he might win.

After a drink of water, Mike panted between breaths. "Coach, I can't get a takedown, he counters everything I try. And he's squeezing my guts out when he's on top."

"Like Allen, huh?"

"Well, Allen was better I think."

"What did we practice?"

"Granby?"

"Right."

"Okay, Coach."

The overtime match was much more controlled than the regular match. First round, no takedown. Noah escaped at the end of the second round. The third round started. Mike hit a beautiful Granby roll, but Noah followed him. Mike hit another Granby and another with Noah right behind. The fourth Granby, however, created enough space and Mike was out, free and tied 1-1 in overtime. Mike looked different this round however. There was no frustration showing on his face. His face was passive, meditative, almost serene. And then in one dramatic effort, Mike shot to both legs of Noah, picked him up and planted him on the mat for a two-point takedown. The whistle blew; the match ended. Mike was state champion. With raised hands, Mike jumped to his feet and leaped across the mat into my arms.

After all the victory laps, Mike shaking his opponent's hand, and coaches shaking hands and congratulating each other on the fine way their wrestlers wrestled, I got Mike aside and asked:

"How did you do it? How did you get that last takedown?"

"I closed my eyes, Coach. I could see his legs better when I closed my eyes."

Mike graduated later that year and to this day is a fine citizen of Homer. Larry Noah in later years coached the Mt. Edgecombe wrestling team which continued to produce fine wrestlers.

Chapter 11

A new teacher often is assigned or somehow volunteered to do a lot of extra things the other teachers don't seem to be doing. That first year I taught sixth-grade P.E., seventh-grade P.E., eight-grade P.E., sixth-grade math, sixth-grade science, and served as high school wrestling coach, junior high wrestling coach, junior high girls track coach and activities director for the junior high. When I had the spare time, I worked weekends on a local sheep farm for a few extra bucks for my growing family. All those activities gave me fond memories and some not so fond.

I enjoyed teaching P.E. Sometimes it was hard to shift gears from classroom teaching to gymroom teaching, but generally it was fun. I enjoyed using innovative games and activities. One game I used with the sixth-grade boys was a mat game called King on the Mat. Everyone got in the middle of the mat and whoever was pushed off the mat had to set out. Whoever was the last person on the mat was the winner. Everyone was against everyone. The sixth-grade girls saw the boys play King on the Mat and wanted to play the same thing during their P.E. class. I said okay.

The girls liked the game so much the first day that they begged to do it another day. I was pleased to relent. I always watched closely to make sure no one was hurt. As I was watching, a couple of girls pushed one girl off the mat, perfectly legal and safe. However, after being pushed off the mat, the young girl burst into tears and ran for the bathroom. Before I could turn my head, every girl in the sixth grade jumped up, bawling her eyes out and heading for the bathroom. I was somewhat perplexed. What could I do? I had no female co-teacher. I was trapped outside the bathroom with no class, all my students were wailing with the most mournful sound. Finally one girl came out. I asked her if anyone was hurt. She scowled and said, "Only her feelings. She was upset that her friends pushed her out."

"Why are the rest crying?" I asked.

"They feel sorry for her."

"Oh."

There were only 15 minutes left in class, so I just let them cry. They seemed all right next period in math, but I never played King on the Mat with that class again.

Another innovative game I had learned in college was a cooperative game where students worked together to scale a wall. I had junior high students so I wanted them to do this same activity, but modify it so there would be little chance for injury. There was an outside wall of the building about 10 feet tall, which seemed just about right. I found an old mat suitable for using outside and put it on the ground to break any fall. If the kids spotted for each other, we would be very safe. I felt I had taken care of every contingency, but I hadn't counted on Bill Divan's mother.

Bill Divan was the tallest kid in the eighth grade. He had grown so fast that his coordination at that age was just not there. I was walking behind him down the hall one day when his left foot turned inward, caught his right ankle and before anyone knew it, both feet flew up in the air higher than my head, and he landed hard on his back. He got up, straightened his glasses and went on down the hall. He was so casual about the whole incident that I guessed things like this must have happened all the time.

Bill was in my P.E. class. We had the wall-climbing activity well on its way. The kids were pulling each other up the wall by rope when the rope slipped and Bill fell. He fell only about three feet and landed on the mat, but as fate would have it, Bill rolled off the mat and scratched his elbow on the gravel. He scratched it pretty bad and got it dirty. It was close to the end of the class, so I sent everyone to the showers while I took Bill to the medicine chest. I cleaned, disinfected and bandaged his elbow. Bill's only concern was if he could wrestle in the junior high match that weekend. He was just as uncoordinated as a wrestler, but I thought nothing could help improve his overall body coordination like wrestling. He worked hard, so I was glad he was on the junior high team.

I looked it over and said that I was sure he could. "It's just a scratch. We might have to bandage it, but it should be fine by this weekend." Bill seemed happy with that statement, and we both went to lunch.

Later I was walking down the hall when Bill's sister saw me and said, "Did you hear what happened to Bill, Mr. Wolfe?"

"No, what happened?"

"He broke his elbow. They had to fly him to Anchorage," she replied.

"Gee, when did that happen?" I asked, thinking he had tripped again.

"It happened in your P.E. class."

"What?" I was exasperated. "He was fine when he went to lunch," I said.

"My mom took him to the doctor and they flew him to Anchorage."

The next three weeks were some of the most miserable in my life. Mrs. Divan came back to Homer telling the school district and the whole town that Bill had broken his elbow when he fell from the wall in my P.E. class. He not only broke his elbow, but he broke the growth plate in his elbow which may stop the growth in his arm and severely handicap him. She was suing the school district for $50,000 and me for $50,000. Fifty thousand dollars was more money that I could imagine, certainly more money than I could count at the time (inflation has since changed that). I knew that my family was surely doomed to financial slavery to the Divan family forever. Every day I dreaded going to school. I just knew the axe would fall that day. I'd talked to the financial director at the school district's central office who said after a formal inquiry and physical examination, the school district was going to pay and I was to be left alone to defend my action in the P.E. class with no support from the school district. After all, I was not a tenured teacher and no P.E. teacher had ever had students climb a wall before.

Bill came back to school the following Monday. No cast on his elbow. "No cast was put on for fear of the swelling from the scratches on my elbow," he told me at our next P.E. class. Bill wore a sling made out of what appeared to be an old curtain. It certainly was not a standard hospital-issue sling. He was seen several times taking his arm out of the sling to stretch it out and often in class he would unconsciously raise his arm well above his head and straighten it out with no apparent pain. When I saw this I called the financial director. He said that Bill's elbow had been x-rayed and they were waiting for the results before they were to take any action on the matter.

Another week dragged by when I again called the central office. "Oh, haven't you heard?" the director said. "We got the x-rays back. We had both elbows x-rayed to compare and our doctor said there was no indication that either elbow had ever been broken, and Mrs. Divan could bring no conflicting doctor's testimony. Bill basically has a scratch on his elbow that is healing nicely. We are not paying a penny to the Divan family. We believe Mrs. Divan is dropping her suit."

It turned out that Mrs. Divan was an almost professional scam artist with lawsuits and very nearly got away with another, taking me and the school district for $100,000. As I thought back about it, I had to say to myself, "Poor Bill." He had to drop out of wrestling, something that he enjoyed doing, and he had to wear publicly that ridiculous sling for well over a month. That was a very cruel thing to do to a young man, and it wasn't a nice thing to do to me either.

I never had a P.E. class climb a wall again, but five years later nearly every P.E. department in the school district, including Homer High School, had a "Project Adventure" class in the curriculum where they engaged in a multitude of climbing activities, including wall-climbing.

Chapter 12

Although my experience with sixth-grade girls was not altogether positive, my work with the girls junior high track team was great. I remember hard-working girls who listened to everything I said and did everything I told them to the best of their ability. Katrina Johansen, a tall, lanky girl who was as reserved a person as you could imagine, ran so hard at the borough championships that she collapsed over the finish line. She was unhurt, but had used every last ounce of strength that she had to finish fourth in the 440-yard run. Her fourth-place finish gave Homer enough points to win. Della Campbell also ran her heart out against very strong opponents to win that same event, and Roberta Rice, a blond bombshell, won several events, including the high jump in which she broke a borough record.

The thing that was most memorable to me was how appreciative the girls were. In the many years of working with boys and young men, I've learned not to expect any thanks until several years after they have graduated from high school. Before that time they figure they have done it all on their own. But these girls were so different. They all would come give me a hug and say things like: "Thanks for pushing us so hard. I couldn't have done so well if it weren't for you."

Roberta was the most expressive. "Oh, this is the best day of my life. We won the borough championships and I got the borough record in high jump. And Coach, if you hadn't told me to change my approach, I'd never have done it. Thank you, thank you, thank you."

A thanks once in a while is the most wonderful award to a coach. I loved working with those girls. Unfortunately it was several years before I had the pleasure of working with girls again.

Being a junior high wrestling coach was rewarding. It was great to see those young kids go out and do battle one-on-one with other equally uncoordinated opponents. The real enjoyment came to me when one of them actually did something I knew I'd taught him. That was always a real "kick in the pants." I never got over that thrill, no matter how many times it happened, no matter how many times one of my wrestlers did it. Wrestling Kenai turned out rather rewarding as well.

Kenai Jr. High had eight times the population that little old Homer had, and they had never lost a dual match in the history of the school. They were quite proud of that record. Kenai kids and coaches bragged about it to the absolute boredom of everyone else. Our first match with them we got killed by their first-string kids; we had two wins out of 16 matches and they were close. Since we had barely enough for one team and they had enough for three teams, we wrestled our wrestlers against them three times. Sometimes our wrestlers got tired, but they were generally in good enough shape to wrestle all three. My kids did win several matches against the second and third teams, and I was proud of their guts and desire.

However, when I walked across the mat to shake hands with the opposing coach, the team score read 84-6 in favor of Kenai, reflecting the varsity or first-team score.

"Boy, you have a crappy team," said Coach Gummer, the Kenai coach. He used a more explicit term than "crappy" and made no attempt to curtail his language in front of the kids of either team.

What he said made me a little hot under the collar, but I replied, "Your kids did a good job," and thought to myself, "Someday I'm going to get even with that jerk, and I think I know just how I'm going to do it."

One month later Kenai came to Homer. My kids were a bit better prepared, so at the end of the first round we were down only 64-12, which meant fewer of our boys were pinned, and we'd won a couple more matches than in the previous match. We started the second round and I had instructed the scorekeeper to just keep adding the score onto the first-round score. This round a few of my kids won, and Coach Gummer came unglued when we started tacking the second-round scores on the first-round scores. He came running to the score table where I met him.

"You can't do that! Your kids have already wrestled once."

"Why?" I asked.

"What do you mean 'why?' It's against the rules."

"Show me where," I said and handed him the rule book.

"You know there's no rules written down about this for junior high. We just never do it that way."

"Well, we do here," I replied.

He threw up his hands and went back to his bench. We started the third round and my first wrestler registered a pin. This score was added onto the team score. He jumped up, clenched his fists, jumped up twice more, clenched his fists again, and muttered under his breath.

This round my wrestlers really shone. They were wrestling Kenai's third string and they registered pin after pin. When the feathers and fur settled, the final Homer pin was tacked onto the team score and Homer had won 136-128, and Kenai had lost its first dual match. They were so mad they refused to shake hands or talk with us after the match. Without showering or even changing clothes, they jumped on their bus and drove the 80 miles home.

As my kids celebrated their dubious victory and showered, I called the newspapers in both Homer and Kenai and reported the team score and a glorious Homer junior high victory. Kenai was a much better team and technically won, but winning is not so much a matter of who won, but more often it's a matter of who thinks they won. Homer's kids thought they won, and that's all that mattered to me. Well, it did matter just a little bit that Coach Gummer lost.

Chapter 13

Nothing much ever happened in math class. We just did math. With the possible exception of the day we got shot.

The class was hard at work on their latest assignment when suddenly the sound of shattering glass erupted, making several of the girls and Mr. Wolfe scream. We looked at the window where a small round hole had appeared. "Someone shot the school!" one of the boys yelled.

"Is everyone all right?" I asked. Everyone looked around. There were bits of glass spread all over the room, but miraculously no one was hurt.

"Mr. Wolfe, here's the bullet." Sure enough a sharp-eyed boy had found the smashed end of a .22-caliber bullet in the wall opposite the windows. He already had his pocket knife out to dig it out.

I reported it to the principal, who called the police. Later a disgruntled high school student who had been expelled from school was arrested for taking pot shots at the school. Apparently we were not the only school room shot at.

When we came to the science unit on Alaska wild animals, I had to tell the class my bear story. I had been working on the weekends for Ed James. Ed's homestead and farm was about 20 miles out East Road, and a couple more across a muskeg. He was getting kind of old and my farm experience helped him out quite a bunch.

One weekend he told me about some sheep that were missing. "I'm sure the coyotes have been killing them, so I drug an old dead cow down in the woods below the path to the west field. I set some traps around, but watch Ol' Blue, the stupid dog got in one yesterday. I've got to go to town, but I should be back in a couple hours. Those tires over there need fixing."

Great. I just loved fixing tires. In truth I'd rather eat nails than do anything like mechanical work, but it came with the territory, so I started fixing the flat tires. I had two tires fixed, four knuckles skinned and had cussed only five times, when I heard Blue howling like the dickens down in the woods right in about the same place the old dead cow must've been. I threw down my tire iron, cussed the sixth time, and stomped down the trail to get Ol' Blue out of the trap. When I got there Blue was not anywhere near the carcass. She was on the other side of the trail howling like death was on her tail. She wasn't caught in any trap. I looked to the right and saw two half-grown brown bear cubs in the ditch. I just had time to think, "Why are they here?" when I saw the mama bear.

She was the size of a horse and she was running as fast as any horse I'd ever seen. An alder branch the size of my leg moved out of her way like grass and she was not making a sound as she ran, but it was obvious I was the object of her haste. Her eyes were red with hate, her fangs were bared and every muscle in her body was straining to get me. She was coming so fast that there was no time to climb any tree. Besides, the flight reflex had already taken over. I was going as fast as my puny human legs would carry me. I felt the mud from her last pounce splatter on my backside. I was trying to figure out what wrestling hold I could use on a bear the size of a horse, but the next pounce didn't come. I looked over my shoulder (still at a dead run) to see that she whirled as quick as a cat and was going after Blue. I continued my dead run up the trail and she almost caught me again before she went back after the dog. I don't think she appreciated either one of us being closer to her cubs than she was.

I made it to Ed's cabin, controlled my heart attack as best I could and loaded Ed's 30-06. Thirty minutes passed before I could talk myself into going out and checking on the dog. I stepped out the door and there was Blue, none the worse for wear. That day I fell in love with Ol' Blue. She's the only dog that ever saved my life. Ed showed up about that time. We both got guns and went down to the dead cow carcass. The tracks were there; the mama's tracks were big enough to almost put both feet in, toe to toe. Just looking at the tracks made your hair stand on end. Ed was surprised.

"I've lived in these parts nigh on to 20 years and never seen any brown bear here before. A few black bear, but never any brownies," he added as he scratched under his hat.

We immediately rounded up the sheep and put them in the barn. They were crowded, but safe. Ed said, "I thought it was moose tearing up the fence. I guess it might have been bear." We walked around the pasture and found several places where the bear had reached up with its front paw and crushed the woven wire fence to the ground. We also found eight sheep carcasses outside the fence covered with brush.

Ed's ranch for the next two weeks was terrorized by the bear. They came in at night and tried to tear boards off the barn to get to the sheep. Ed had an old Datsun pickup with a sheepskin inside the cab. The bear broke in the side window, ripped off the door and got the sheepskin.

I came out after school to help Ed put up spotlights so he could shoot her if he saw her and at the least would protect his animals at night. I also came out the next weekend to help Ed put up a powerful electric wire around the top of his pasture fence. About that time it snowed and there were no more signs of bear.

Of course, in sixth-grade science class I had to tell my bear story much to the pleasure and entertainment of the students. Soon the story was all over town in several variations. Everyone in town was talking about the brown bear so close to Homer. One night I received a call from the local game warden.

"Can you get a message to Ed James? Ask him to drop by the Fish and Game office when he's in town. I want to talk to him about his bear problem."

"Okay," I said. "I can reach him on the CB most nights."

A few weeks later Ed told me about his meeting with the game warden:

"Come in, Ed, and sit down," the game warden invited. "I understand you've got some brown bear problem."

"Ya' got that right," drawled Ed.

"Well, we're going to take care of that bear for you. We'll be right out to capture her and haul her off."

"Her cubs too?"

"Her cubs too!"

"Well, I'm mighty glad to hear that. I'd like you to come pronto," said Ed. "'Cause I don't want to have to kill her, but I will to protect my livestock."

"No, no, no, you can't do that," the game warden said gravely, shaking his head. "That animal is the property of the state of Alaska."

"Oh," replied Ed, "I was wondering who owned that animal. Ya' see, I've been wondering who I could charge for my eight dead sheep."

"Oh, no, no, you can't charge us for that," said the game warden.

"Well, if I can't, then I guess you don't really own that bear, do you?" And with that, Ed left.

The bear never did come back to the area, maybe because Ed stopped raising sheep. Ed also said that he never saw any Game Department people up there. He rather doubts anyone would be dumb enough to try to capture three bears that big.

Chapter 14

My wife and I had agreed when we got married to have a family. We felt that to have a good family, we needed a full-time homemaker. Nina had spent a number of years in the workforce and now happily volunteered for that position. I therefore became the bread-winner. A schoolteacher's salary is not extravagant, but sufficient if I also worked all summer. The first full summer, through Al Poindexter, I was able to get a job at a sawmill. I'd never worked in a sawmill, but was told the most important qualification one needed was a strong back. The sawmill was across Kachemak Bay at a small inlet called Jakalof Bay. It would mean that I would have to be away from home nearly the whole summer. However, if we made as much as we expected, we could probably put aside enough money to put a down payment on a home and move out of the Stinking Hole. So we determined to make the sacrifice that summer.

Working at the sawmill was an interesting experience filled with interesting characters. Bill, the sawyer, was never a good friend of mine. He soon learned of my conservative nature. This tall, lanky Arkansanian in his lanky southern drawl at lunchtime and coffee breaks drawled out one risque joke after another. I hated his jokes and let him know so, but he enjoyed irritating me with them. I hated his jokes all summer, but somehow I admired his ability to remember so many. For the entire summer he told dirty jokes one right after another all lunch break and most coffee breaks, and never repeated the same one.

Vern was another character. He must have been in his late 60s. He weighed about 115 pounds, but was an electric crane operator, which needed little strength. His arms were about as big around as a broomstick, his legs not much bigger. He shaved and bathed every couple weeks. Al, who had worked at the sawmill several summers, told me why Vern still worked at the mill. It seemed that Vern had won the Tanana Ice Classic several years earlier and was a rich man.

"What is the Tanana Ice Classic?" I asked.

Al proceeded to explain. "Up near Fairbanks there is a river which, like many of the rivers of an area that far north, freezes thick with ice. But in the spring the ice does not gradually melt away as it does in a lake, but in one mighty crash it breaks up and moves down the stream en masse. It never happens the same day or time, so each year all over Alaska the city of Tanana promotes a sweepstakes for charity. All over Alaska and I guess even in the Lower 48 states people pay a couple of dollars to guess the time that the ice breaks up on the Tanana River. The prize is often several hundred thousand dollars."

"So Vern won it," I said. "That's great. Why is he working here?"

"Well, the way I understand it is that a lawyer up in Fairbanks volunteered to help every winner with his taxes, so a winner won't have to pay all his winnings in taxes. One of the things Vern has to do is to keep working at his job for five years. He's still got a couple years to go." I had noticed that Vern was never very excited about payday. Now I knew why.

Cecil was a big raw-boned cowboy. He had grown up in Alaska on one of the several ranches in the Homer area. He was every bit a cowboy from his dirty old black cowboy hat to his Charlie Pride tapes. He was as fine a friend as a person could have, but you also knew it was not a good idea to cross him. He was as tough as that tough life had made him. We were roommates and good friends. He didn't hold a grudge, even when I pushed him in the bay on his birthday. But darn he was stubborn. He would never back down on an argument. He even lost two tires over one of his arguments.

It happened one morning as we were eating breakfast.

"You hear that Floyd woke up this morning to four flat tires?" Sonny added to the conversation.

"No. You don't say?" Cecil answered. "How did that happen?"

"No one rightly knows, they weren't cut or slashed or anything like that."

"Probably someone shot 'em," I said.

"No one shot 'em. Everyone in camp would have heard that. Floyd's house is only a hundred yards away," Cecil insisted.

"Well, they could have used a .22."

"What do you mean? Floyd has 10-ply steel-belted radials. A .22 wouldn't touch them," Cecil came right back.

"I don't know," I said. "I was shot once with a .22 out hunting. It felt pretty powerful to me."

"You can't tell me that a .22 would even faze those tires. Floyd's tires are just like mine, and it would take a lot more than a .22 to flatten them," Cecil argued.

Most of the guys had been around Cecil a lot longer than I had, and they recognized a chance to push him into a real argument. So one at a time each of the guys at the table sided with me, extolling the power of the .22.

"I'll prove it," Cecil finally said. We followed him out to his truck and he pulled out his Colt .22 revolver. He pointed it at his front tire. Bamm! He pointed it at his back tire. Bamm! When the second blast stopped reverberating from the hills, all we could hear was the double pssssst from each of Cecil's tires as they slowly went flat in front of us.

Cecil stood there with a surprised look on his face. "I guess a .22 is a little more powerful than I thought." It took Cecil several hours to fix both tires after work that night.

"I didn't think I'd ever need a spare with those truck tires, and now I have to fix two flats in the same day," Cecil admitted to me later that evening. He did buy a spare later, I think.

The sawmill was owned by a Japanese company and somehow because it was owned by a foreign firm it did not have to live up to rigid U.S. safety standards. There were several accidents, and the most serious was my fault.

I was just a laborer at the mill. I did what they told me to do. A lot of what I did involved being on the hard end of a shovel, but it was good money. Al Poindexter, my good buddy and assistant coach, had worked his way up to the position of "offbearer" which was a little more money, but a lot more dangerous. An offbearer stood beside two giant circular saws which cut slabs from three- to six-foot diameter logs. Sawdust, water, tree juice and splinters flew everywhere. Slabs weighing some-times as much as a man fell from the logs, which the offbearer must direct in one of the various manners to the conveyor belt and thus onto the burner where all the sawdust and slabs were burned. The offbearer not only directed the slabs, but also had the responsibility of pushing the correct button to direct the cants (which were the final product of the sawmill) to the cranes to be stacked, ready for shipping to Japan.

It amazed me that anyone would want to do a job so intense and risky of death and injury. Al did a good job at it, until one day a giant slab fell right on him. He twisted his leg and in other ways was injured so that he needed to be sent by plane to the hospital in Homer.

The boss looked around, saw me and said, "You, you're the new offbearer. This button kicks the cants off to the right, this one to the left. This button puts up the stop to keep the logs from going off into the conveyor. Understand?"

I understood what he said, but I was not sure that I had been prop-erly in-serviced to this position, so I answered, "Uh huh."

"If you get in trouble, pound on the saw cage and the sawyer will stop sawing. Okay?"

Now that I understood. I knew I could be all right if I had that kind of a safety valve. "Okay," I answered, and we were off sawing logs again. My initial fear of the dangerous conditions I was working under did not lessen. Soon a slab jammed in the conveyor belt, making it impossible to get rid of any more slabs.

I pounded on the saw cage and went to help Craig Poindexter, Al's brother, unjam the slabs. We were busily working when to our horror the sawyer sawed another slab and dumped a cant on the rollers. No one had told me how to turn the rollers off or how to keep the stop up whenever I was not at my position, so the cant rolled out and fell, all 3,000 pounds, on Craig. The end of this big log landed right on Craig's leg, breaking it and trapping him in the conveyor. The conveyor began carrying the cant and Craig up to be dumped into the fiery burner. I had not been told how to turn anything off, but I knew where the "off" buttons were. I leaped across the moving roller and hit every off button I could find in hopes I would turn off the conveyor. I did hit the right button and at the same time attracted a lot of attention since I had turned off the entire mill.

I hurried back to Craig. He was screaming in pain. The end of the log was crushing his leg. Vern was already there, trying to figure out how to get the 3,000-pound log off Craig.

I was so scared, spurred on by the screams of agony and my own guilt, that I grabbed the end of the three-foot-diameter green spruce log and lifted. It never entered my head that to lift that much weight was impossible. Up came the end of the log.

"Get him out of there," I yelled. Vern pulled Craig out. When Craig was free, I set the log down and picked him up in my arms and carried him down the conveyor.

Craig screamed between sobs. "Look at my leg, it's broke! I'll never be able to run again!" Craig was one of the premiere high school runners in the state. His leg looked like a limp noodle. He must've broken it pretty bad because there was no stiffness in any of it.

"You'll run again," I said. "I've broken both of these arms and I'm carrying you in them."

With that statement, Craig settled right down and took the rest of the ordeal stoically. The plane that took Al over to Homer turned right around to pick up Craig.

It was the next day before I realized that I had done the impossible. I'd heard about little old ladies who had lifted up cars in times of stress. I know now what that's like. I got that burst of energy from just plain fear. I thought sure the whole situation was my fault and I felt at that moment that I had to do something about it. It was just one of those crazy once-in-a-lifetime things.

The mill workers and loggers in camp somehow thought different. They called me "Mr. Wolfe" from that point on. I felt like I was back at school. Also, Bill, the sawyer, didn't tell quite so many dirty jokes around me.

Both Al and Craig recovered fully, and Craig continued to be a great runner. I was so glad Al came back two weeks later. I got used to the constant terror of the offbearer position. I didn't get used to the fact that the water used to keep the saws cool kept my hands wet constantly, and I hated touching anything with water-wrinkled hands.

Chapter 15

Moving logs to Japan from Alaska was quite an undertaking. After the logs were run through the mill they were put in bundles, then a raft of bundles was anchored in the bay. When enough logs were prepared, a ship would anchor just outside Jakalof Bay and rafts of logs would be towed up to the ship. The ship's cranes would lift the bundles to be stored in and on the ship.

When a log ship came in, all work at the mill shut down. Mill workers and some of the loggers were needed as workers to load the ship. There was always an air of excitement about a ship coming in. I didn't really know what the excitement was all about, but I could feel it from everyone. There was a quickness in people's voices when they talked about the ship coming in. Nearly all the stories about the mill and workers that used to work there seemed to be centered on when the "ship came in."

When the ship finally did come in, I saw why there was so much excitement. It was the rodeo of the ocean. There is something deep down inside most men that makes them enjoy something just a little independent, just a little harder than usual and with just enough excitement in it — excitement like barely dodging opportunities of death and mutilation. Loading a log ship was all of that and spiced with opportunities to help and/or see some of your fellow workers get wet.

There were not enough mill workers and loggers to load the log ship, so longshoremen from various places in the state and various other hardy part-time workers would be flown in for the week of loading. Everyone got a bit more pay and bonuses for getting the ship loaded quickly, but the best part of loading the ship was that they brought to camp Leroy Long and his wife to cook that week.

And what cooks they were! Every morning we had our choice of oatmeal with honey and cinnamon, pancakes of every style, French toast with side orders of bacon, eggs, sausage and my favorite — biscuits and gravy with big chunks of ham. Every homemade pastry was fresh and hot right out of the oven, and for drinks we had gallons of milk, apple juice and orange juice. All you could eat was the order of the day.

We packed big lunches as everything we needed for a great lunch was right there. At night they always served a great meal like pork chops with lots of gravy, rice and several vegetables. Wednesday night was steak night with great baked Alaskan potatoes, smothered in butter and sour cream. And of course, fresh salad, that I usually smothered in Thousand Island dressing. Every night was a culinary delight in a down-home sorta' way. For dessert we had pies: pumpkin, coconut cream, blueberry, apple, all freshly baked. The desert was left out on the serving table until about midnight for snacks. When the ship came in, the food Leroy and his wife cooked was worth getting excited about.

Working the ship was an adventurous affair. You got up in time to catch the transport barge that ferried you out to the ship. Once on the ship, the crew was divided into two groups: the ship workers and the raft workers. The raft workers were the most prestigious. Wearing heavy clog boots they would climb down the rope ladder from the deck of the ship sometimes 50 feet to their work on the log rafts. They stayed on the rafts all day except at breaks and lunch. The raft men usually climbed the ladder to the deck at break time, but just to show off, they had races up and down. Some climbed up the ladder with no feet just to be macho. Everyone wanted to be on the rafts except those of us who weren't that good at climbing up and down ropes. Raft work also gave those who worked there the opportunity to slip off the logs and get wet, which was all kinds of fun in the 40-degree Fahrenheit water of Kachemak Bay. A dip in the ocean in Alaska is even more fun for everyone who sees someone fall in. Even when we couldn't see the raft men, it was no more than 10 seconds after someone fell in the water that through the gossip line everyone on the ship knew about it.

Occasionally, on a hot day, a few guys would purposely take a dip, but they had to be strange. Water at that temperature usually causes hypothermia in about four minutes. Once, Pete, a hippie from Seldovia, dived several times 70 feet off the crow's nest to the water. Of course, everyone said he was on marijuana when he did it.

The mode of operation went like this: the crane operator would lower two cables to the raft men who would take the cable end in one hand, the hook in another and loop the cable under and around a bundle of logs. Then they would step onto another bundle and wait for the crane to haul the bundle out of the water to the hold of the ship. The workers on the ship unhooked the bundles. The work in the hold didn't sound hazardous, but in fact it was the most dangerous. The bundles of wood were lowered by the crane and placed in the hold, where hold men had to keep out of the way of the swinging bundles. This was not especially hard in good weather, but when the weather turned foul, so did the lives of the hold men. The ship swayed back and forth, making footing unstable. The slings from the crane also swayed, which started a wave action that traveled down the sling and terminated at the bundle. The whipping motion of the bundle made it impossible to know where the bundle was going to be at any given time. It was only the skill of the crane operator that kept the hold men from becoming red stains on the side of the hold. There were just no places to hide from those bundles in the hold of the ship.

Once a bundle was in the right place and unhooked, the hold men faced a new danger. To pull the cables out from under the logs, the wench had to strain until the end knob was pulled free. The end of each cable always popped out so hard that the 20-pound nubs at the end of cable snaked all over the hold. Us hold men soon learned to find some hiding place from those unpredictable snakes. If either one of them made hard contact with a hold man, it would inflect serious damage, maybe death. Sometimes you'd swear they were alive and would even follow you right into your hole. A few hold men got hurt, but only a few, and we just kept loading logs.

It still amazes me that the more of those floating logs you put in the ship the deeper the ship sank. Floating logs should make the ship float better, but they sank it. There's some physics principle that explains it, and I think I had someone explain it to me once, but it's still amazing to me.

As long as the weather was nice, things usually went great, but when the weather was bad, then everything was bad. The boat began rocking so that about half the crew started getting sick. When the crane operators (or "wench men" as they were called) were sick, they had to keep working, but they didn't care nearly as much about the hold men. Some of the hold men were so sick they didn't care that the wench men didn't care. Down in the hold there was not even a good place to throw up.

At the end of the bad-weather day, everyone was so glad to see the ferry coming to get us, and cheers went up everywhere. The bad weather was not done with us, however. The waves were pitching everything around so that we couldn't get the ramp close to the ferry. The raft men finally came to our rescue by deciding to climb down the rope ladder and running across the log raft to meet the ferry. That was a little dangerous to say the least, with logs pitching everywhere, but when a few made it, everyone was over the side of the ship and running toward the ferry. No one wanted to be on that ship another minute, and land was only a half hour away. Miraculously, everyone made it safely.

Weather conspired against us again one night. The waves were crashing so hard against the beach that the landing-craft ferry couldn't get close to the beach. After cruising off-beach for at least an hour, all of us were even more sick. Finally, some logger on the beach fired up a D-9 Caterpillar and drove it out in the waves as far as he could and ferried us, eight at a time, back and forth from ferry to beach. Eight people are all that can hang onto the cabin of a D-9 Cat. We know, we tried to get more. Somehow we all made it safely to the beach and I think all of us kissed the solid ground. A funny thing about sea sickness. When you get back on solid ground, it's gone. All of us sick guys in the 100-yard walk to the mess hall just got hungry as all heck for Leroy's beef stew and biscuits, and all of us ate a healthy bit of them that night.

Friday night we had fresh halibut. Leroy had done it right. He had deep-fried it in his own special batter with a side dish of the best homemade tartar sauce. Halibut is the best fish in the world. I know a lot of Southern catfish lovers and English cod lovers would like to argue with me, but they wouldn't argue long if I could give them a taste of fresh Kachemak Bay halibut cooked by Leroy Long.

After I ate my third helping and let out my belt the second time, it was time to feel bad. Not that I'd eaten so much, that was worth it. It was time to feel bad toward Floyd, our boss.

The story behind why we had fresh halibut at camp began a week earlier. Sonny and Vern had come to me one day after work.

"Steve, would you like to go halibut fishing with us?" Sonny asked.

They knew that they had me hooked with that question. Since coming over to Jakalof Bay I'd caught the fishing fever my dad always had. Salmon were everywhere. It didn't take a lot of patience to catch one and it was a whole lot of fun tying into a 10- to 20-pound fish that fought you until your arms were tired. I couldn't get enough. I was fishing until 1 a.m. after work, and at breaks in work I'd cast a few in the surf. I had so many salmon I didn't know what to do with them until Vern showed me how to smoke them. But I'd never fished for halibut. However, I was game.

"Yah. When?" I was ready to go that minute.

"Well," Vern said, "we're going to set a skate out in the mouth of Jakalof tonight if you want to come along. We have the skate and the bait. We're going after dinner and if you help us, we'll share the catch."

"That sounds great to me. I'd love to go. Thanks." Something in the back of my mind said, "Look out, something's going on." These guys were fellow workers and could be considered friends, but it was unusual for them to ask me along on any of their activities.

After dinner we walked down to the beach to the boat and then I saw why I'd been invited. It was a row boat. I doubt Vern had strength enough to lift one oar out of the water, let alone two, and Sonny liked his beer and his belly was as rotund as his bald head, just bigger. He was certainly strong enough to row, but his strength was not in the endurance category.

We loaded up and I took the position I knew I was supposed to and began rowing. Vern and Sonny were really friendly and, except for the tediousness of rowing across Jakalof Bay for an hour, it was pleasant. In summer the sun goes down for a couple hours, but it doesn't get dark. It's just twilight all evening. That summer evening, out on the water, listening to friends chat away, hearing the gentle slap, slap, swoosh of the water against the boat was rather a nice experience. On I rowed as Vern and Sonny discussed the best place to put out the skate, and gave me directions where to row.

A halibut skate is a series of hooks tied to stout line, baited, anchored at one end and tied to a buoy at the other. The hooks generally stay on the bottom where the halibut feed. The skate is left out for a period of time and then retrieved with any fish the skate has caught.

We found a place that Vern felt was just right. Vern was pretty smart about things like that, so Sonny agreed. We tossed out the big rock that was the skate anchor, tied off the buoy and headed for home. I rowed for another hour as Sonny and Vern finished their six-pack. We all had a good time on the way back. I convinced myself that I liked to work that hard and that it was good for me, but I sure wasn't looking forward to rowing back out to check the line.

On Saturday, Floyd, the boss, pulled into camp with his 18-foot motor boat because a ship was coming in that day and he had to be there to oversee the anchoring. Everyone could have done everything without him, but we always let him tell us what to do so he'd feel important.

Sonny was quick to see the advantage of the motorboat though. He quickly asked Floyd if he'd check our halibut skate when he went out to meet the ship. Floyd was a little reluctant, but agreed to do so.

That night just about suppertime Floyd came in with his boat just whooping and hollering.

"One hundred and thirty pounds!" he yelled. We ran to the dock and sure enough he had a big fish. The biggest I'd ever seen in my life to that point.

"I weighed it on the ship, and if you think this is big, you should have seen the other two, 156 pounds and 202 pounds. The Japanese on the ship were excited when I gave them those fish."

"What?" I blurted out. Vern kicked me right in the back of the leg. I shut up, but was a bit perturbed that Floyd would steal our fish and give them away without asking.

Sonny and Vern accepted their fish with grim faces and Floyd didn't notice they were not nearly as happy about the situation as he was. We hauled the fish up to the cook shack and the cook put it in the freezer for us. We decided we'd share it with the camp. Then Vern said, "Sorry I kicked you, but Floyd would have just fired you if you'd called him on that. He's like that." Vern added a few choice expletives about the boss and continued:

"He was just brown-nosing with the Japanese bosses on the ship and he didn't give a damn whose fish he did it with."
We rowed out a couple more times to check the skate and we caught a few fish, but none of them were close to the size of those first three.

The summer finally ended, I collected my last paycheck and we moved into a new Farm Home-financed house that was to be our home for 20 years. We almost tearfully left the Stinking Hole. Well, not exactly tearfully.

Chapter 16

A new school year started and I had some new assignments. They were the same as my old assignments, except now I was teaching all seventh- and eight-grade math, as well as physical education, and serving as junior high activities director. I enjoyed teaching math. It was a subject you could set goals for your students and measure those goals. I set a goal to have my math students average in the 75th percentile on the SRA tests. The nationwide average was the 50th percentile, but I wanted them 25 percentile points above that average. Four years later, the last year that I taught all the junior high math students, my eighth-graders averaged in the 74th percentile and my seventh-graders in the 76th percentile. I figured that was close enough.

Being activities director for the junior high meant that generally I was in charge of dances. I didn't mind that assignment at all. I loved to dance and this was the "disco era." A lot of negative comments have been made about disco, but what I noticed is that no one stood on the sides. Everyone danced and seemed to have a good time. Both girls and boys asked others to dance with them. I always thought that the custom of boys being the only ones to ask someone to dance was dumb. If a girl wanted to dance, she ought to have the right to ask someone to dance with her, and sure enough those junior high girls did, and so everyone danced. I was even asked to dance. I think those junior high dances of the disco era were the most enjoyable dances I ever attended. The carnival — now that was another story.

"We want this carnival to be the best ever," Dale said in the student council meeting. "It's our big fund-raiser of the year, so we need everyone there." Dale was tall for an eighth-grader, handsome and well-liked by the students. He was bright and considered kind of a "nerd" by the kids, but not too much of a nerd. "So here's the plan," he continued. Every time I heard that phrase from Dale I knew I, as activities director, was going to get in trouble somehow. Dale rummaged behind the table and pulled out the most realistic gorilla costume I'd ever seen. "What's a carnival without a gorilla? We'll use him to advertise and for excitement at the carnival. Everyone will come to see the live gorilla."

"Yah, but who's going to wear it?" All eyes turned to me and I knew that this was one of those times I should have kept my mouth shut.

"Why, you, Coach Wolfe," Dale smiled back.

"You kind of look like a gorilla anyway," said Cindy.

"Great. Now I really want to wear that costume."

"You'll be great, Coach," said Greg.

"It looks like I'm not going to get out of this. Okay. What do I have to do?"

Dale outlined his ideas for advertising the carnival. As I got into the idea, like mold, it kind of grew on me. Probably everyone has a fantasy about being King Kong. This was my chance to live out that fantasy. Mr. Loosely grinned as Dale explained what he wanted to do and asked if we could take an afternoon to do it.

"I'll be glad to take Mr. Wolfe's classes for the afternoon," Mr. Loosely continued to grin. "This sounds fun."

With that permission, I donned the gorilla suit and drove Dale and Cindy over to Paul Banks Elementary School the following Thursday. You should have seen the heads turn when people saw a gorilla driving a Volkswagen bug through the main streets of Homer.

I'd practiced all week to perfect the gorilla walk, much to the giggles and delight of my three kids Ivan, Rebekah and Nina. They liked to see Daddy walking sideways and dragging his knuckles. My wife said I ought to practice more because she didn't notice any difference between what I was doing and my regular gait.

With the costume came a thick leather collar and chain. When we got to the elementary school, Dale took hold of the chain and we walked into the first class, announced the carnival and the surprise visitor, at which time I leapt from the door to the top of the nearest table, growling and pounding my chest. I didn't realize how truly frightening the costume was. It seemed like 10,000 little kids were screaming in abject terror. They clawed at the windows and dived under the nearest desks where they had company because their teacher and Cindy had screamed just as loud and dived for cover as well. Only Dale kept his cool.

The kids' reaction was so pronounced that I stopped growling. One by one heads popped from under desks until I growled again, they screamed again and dived for cover again. Eventually all the kids saw that I was not "real" and came out for a better inspection. Dale gave his pitch about the carnival, Cindy helped the teacher out from under her desk and we went to the next classroom where the same scene was repeated. Dale felt we made a great impression. Cindy thought we might have scared all the kids away, but Dale said they'd come and bring all their friends.

Dale was right, as usual. The carnival was packed and 90 percent of the kids stood wide-eyed watching me at a safe distance as I growled, pounded my chest and scratched. The junior high and high school kids came also and had to have their picture taken with me. I settled down long enough to let pictures be taken of me with my arms around the older students.

Eventually little kids got brave enough to have their pictures taken with the gorilla. The carnival was a hit, and the junior high pulled in three times the money of any previous carnival. There was enough money from that one activity to run nearly every student activity the rest of the year.

Chapter 17

"Mr. Wolfe, could I leave these baby guppies with you today?" It was Kurt asking the question. He was one of my seventh-grade math students. Kurt was a nice kid. Not one of the best math students, but certainly not one of the worst. At the moment his face was etched with concern.

"Why did you bring them to school?" I asked.

"My momma guppy had babies and the lady at the pet store said she'd buy them. So I'm taking them over to her after school." Kurt always had some money-making project going on.

Kurt had short-cropped wiry blond hair, a natural cream-colored tan skin and angular handsomeness. His natural pleasant looks, coupled with his desire to make money, could have turned him into a real hustler. But Kurt also had a kind heart, which kept him pretty straight.

I peered at the plastic sack he held. It was full of water and about a thousand little fish. They looked like transparent tails propelling two huge eyes through the water-filled sack. Every once in a while one would stop and peer back at me with those big eyes. They reminded me of the eyes of a fawn, so trusting, so sad and helpless. To see one look at you with those sad eyes was enough to win anyone's heart.

"Sure, put them over there on the counter." I pointed to a safe place.

"Thanks, Mr. Wolfe. I'll get them after school." And Kurt was gone.

That was Friday. After school I stayed around for about an hour and a half in my room, getting ready for the next week. It never occurred to me that Kurt never came to get his guppies. I locked up the room and went home for the weekend with not a guppy on my mind.

Monday came however, and the first thing I saw when I entered my room was the plastic sack of little fish. There was still plenty of water in the sack, but the guppies were immobile and unresponsive. Most of them were floating upside down near the surface. I immediately called the pet store. Dorothy Johnson, the pet store owner, was sympathetic but gave me the bad news. "No, I'm sure they're dead. That long without movement of the water probably depleted all the oxygen out of the water. It is sure a shame all those guppies died." I had to agree as I looked at those big sad guppy eyes floating in the stagnant water.

"Kurt, all your guppies are dead." I gave him my sternest look when he came to my room later that morning. "You didn't pick them up on Friday."

"Oh, no, I forgot." He looked at the bag of dead guppies and his 13-year-old heart melted. I could see he genuinely cared for those fish and felt terrible they'd all died.

"Well, now you have to get rid of them. They were your responsibility and now you must take care of them," I said.

"Kurt, I'll help," Darren put in. Darren was a friend to everyone and always was there to help anyone who seemed to need it. A look of relief crept over Kurt's face and the boys left the room with the plastic sack, water and guppies.

They talked it over and decided the best way to get rid of the dead fish was to flush them down the toilet. So they walked into the boys' bathroom and solemnly dumped them into the commode.

To their horror, as soon as the guppies hit the water of the toilet all came instantly alive and began happily swimming around. Kurt and Darren panicked. They began shouting and trying to get the guppies back. They tried to dip them out of the toilet with their hands, but the fish were too fast, slippery and small. They managed to stir up quite a commotion and get each other quite wet with toilet water, when they decided to have Darren stay guard so no one would use the toilet and Kurt ran frantically to the principal's office.

Mrs. Meyers, the combination secretary-nurse, was there for just such emergencies.

"My guppies are in the toilet! Do you have something I could get them out with?" Kurt shouted at the top of his lungs and then at the same volume shouted the whole story to her.

Mrs. Meyers began laughing. Kurt was almost in tears and Mr. Loosely, the principal, stepped out of his cubicle to see what was going on. He was not amused.

"What would your parents say if they knew I let you play in the toilet? Flush the fish down." And Mr. Loosely followed Kurt into the boys' bathroom to make sure the deed was done, all the time wondering how he ever got to be a junior high principal.

Kurt and Darren told me about it later.

"Mr. Wolfe, I think every eye of every guppy was looking at me when I pulled the lever, and they kept watching me as they swirled around and down. The worst thing was that two of them swam back to the top and I had to flush them twice."

"Well, Kurt, I know that you feel bad about having to flush them, but I'll bet if those guppies were tough enough to live in that sack all weekend, they're probably tough enough to live in the sewer," I consoled.

Kurt immediately brightened up. "Yah, you're right, Mr. Wolfe." With that happy thought, Kurt and Darren left, guppies no longer a worry.

Chapter 18

All the fun at school was not with the kids. There was quite a bit of fun among the faculty as well. Practical jokes abounded. I wasn't particularly good at doing practical jokes, but one time I thought I came up with a pretty good one.

I brought in some health food cookies that Nina had seen made on TV. They looked great, but tasted awful. Faculty lounges are notorious. Bring anything in: stale donuts, whatever, if there is no sign on it to keep away, everything will be devoured in no time. These cookies were really bad, but I thought that even they would be eaten by the teachers. I brought in a dozen and put them on the faculty table. We had eight faculty members on the staff. Eight cookies were taken that day, two others disappeared when the janitors came on that night. The last two cookies stayed uneaten for the next two weeks. They disappeared only after we had two substitute teachers come on for a day. They were bad cookies.

Most of the practical jokes seemed to come from McLuen. He was the pool director. I don't think he had a lot to do all day, so he spent his time pulling practical jokes on people. He had nailed about everyone when he finally got me.

He came in one night and put Limburger cheese under the heater of the coach's office during wrestling season. When I got up to the office and turned on the heater the most gad-awful smell reeked from everywhere. I could not figure where it was coming from. I opened the door, checked the vents for dead mice and generally took the room apart looking for something rotten. The only thing I could find was a pair of my old wrestling shoes and I thought they had to be the source of the smell. I must've looked funny carrying my wrestling shoes at arm's length, holding my nose all the way down the hallway to the outside dumpster. But the smell didn't go away.

It just happened to be one of those rare days when the superintendent stopped by the school. He stepped in the door of the school and said, "Smells like Limburger cheese." When he said that, I knew it was McLuen and where to look for what. It wasn't long before I had the awful mess cleaned up, but the coach's office reeked for months.

The principal's office door opened in and the vice-principal's office opened out. It was that oddity that must have spawned McLuen's two most famous practical jokes.

One morning the vice-principal opened his door to be smothered by a mound of crinkled newspaper. His whole room had been filled with newspaper, not halfway up, but all the way to the ceiling. It took Mr. Naughty and the custodians an hour and a half to clean it all out. Us faculty members thought it was as funny as a rubber crutch, but Mr. Loosely wasn't laughing. He couldn't open his office door. He could unlock it, but it wouldn't open. The custodians shoved, used crowbars, tried to take apart the hinges, everything, but they couldn't open it. This office had no windows or other openings so no one knew what to do.

Everyone knew McLuen had done this, but Loosely was never going to give in and ask him how he did it. So Mr. Loosely set up shop with the secretary while the custodians tried to open his door. About noon someone told someone to tell someone to tell the janitors to go through the roof. The most agile custodian was then boosted up and was able from the hallway to go up through the ceiling tile over the wall and down through the ceiling tile of the office. McLuen had used the same method to get into both offices to do his dirty deeds. A 2-by-4 board was braced under the doorknob and against the desk, making it impossible to open the door from the outside.

It was a couple months before Loosely and Naughty got revenge, but when they did, they did it right.

Tom McLuen had one duty he took very seriously. He was senior class sponsor, which meant he had to help the seniors with all their traditional festivities on the limited senior class budget.

Tom this year went to the home economics teacher, Mrs. Spyder, and asked her if her home economics class could make up the hors d'oeuvres and dinner for the senior prom. He thought sure this would save the senior class money.

Mrs. Spyder agreed, but when Ron Naughty heard about the arrangement, the old light bulb went on in his head. He got Mrs. Spyder, Diane Wayland, the bookkeeper and Mr. Loosely together for a conference and they hatched the following plan that worked like clockwork.

First Mrs. Spyder submitted a bill to Diane asking for 10 times the amount of money she really needed. This was four times the entire senior class total funds. Diane called Tom into her office and asked him about it. He was flabbergasted.

"What am I going to do?" he asked Diane.

"Well, I could transfer some funds around and help you out, but what do I get in return?" Diane replied.

"What do you want?" asked Tom.

"My friends and I would really like to use the school swimming pool, late Saturday night sometime. Can you arrange that?"

"Sure!" Tom said, relieved that he wouldn't have that awful financial burden on his senior class.

"I want that promise in writing," said Diane.

Tom thought that was an unusual request, but wrote out a letter giving Diane and her friends access to the pool the next Saturday evening, in consideration for her help with the senior budget deficit, and signed it. The next day Tom, Diane and Ron were all called into Mr. Loosely's office.

"What is this I found in the copy room?" Mr. Loosely shoved across the desk to Tom and Diane the signed letter of permission. Diane was a great actress, one of the best in the local theater group. She turned white as a sheet on cue.

"Did you write this, Tom?" Mr. Loosely continued in his best trial lawyer voice.

"Well, yah."

"Did you, Diane, accept this arrangement? And why?"

Diane humbly explained the arrangement.

"According to Section 44, Article B of the State Statutes," (Mr. Loosely was making these numbers up), "Diane, you have broken the law in your employment. There is no other recourse than to dismiss you from your position."

Diane immediately burst into tears, something she was famous for doing in local theatrical circles. Tom was just beside himself. "That's not fair to Diane. I thought it was unusual, but how can she lose her job over using the swimming pool?"

Unruffled, Mr. Loosely continued, "Tom, you have not broken any state law, as you probably know, but you have certainly compromised the ethical agreements a teacher adheres to. Have you read those ethical agreements?"

"I think so," replied Tom.

"If you will look at page 176 in the last paragraph," (again the page number and reference were made up), "you'll see that what you have done could cost you your job as a teacher and bar you from further service for the remainder of your life," Mr. Loosely finished.

"But all I was trying to do was save the senior class some money," cried out Tom. He was sweating under the collar at this point.

"I realize that," continued Mr. Loosely, "but this is a matter of ethics. I will have to consult with Superintendent Cannon before I can proceed further."

Diane wailed and sobbed some more.

"I have to let Mr. Cannon know that you have been informed of your infraction, so could you sign this paper indicating I have informed you of it?" Mr. Loosely shoved another piece of paper across the desk to Tom, with a pen.

The paper read:

*Tom McLuen, you have just been
taken for the ride of your life.*

_____

sign here

"What!" yelled Tom and everyone in the room burst into laughter, even Diane. Tom's face turned scarlet. The blood slowly drained from his face, and then even he chuckled a bit, but I understand he was a little too relieved to laugh real hard. That ended the practical jokes for a time.

Chapter 19

Wrestling season was again fast-approaching. We'd had preseason workouts and before the snow came we played flag football. The kids loved it and often it deteriorated into tackle football. To keep it structured, I put together a couple games with Ninilchik, a high school only 40 miles away. We went up there and they came down to Homer for a fun game at each place. Our first game we played at their field.

We were much better organized and Ninilchik had fewer kids, so we won pretty easily 20-8. They scored when we let their fast Indian boy get around our end and run a touchdown.

The second game in Homer was not nearly so easy. They learned to use their strength. They would pitch out to the tall lanky Indian boy and let him run. There is no substitute for speed in football, and this boy could run like a deer. It was only after a full team effort that we were able to keep the score down.

Our quarterback happened to be an Indian also. Robert Necklace was obviously Indian, but where he got that bright red hair I never found out. The thing I was most interested in was his quarterbacking ability. He was pretty fair at doing that; he could throw well and most of all he did exactly what I told him to do, even when that was not exactly what I wanted him to do.

Just before the end of the game and trailing by 11 points, during a time-out I gave him a play sequence.

"Robert, I want you to hand-off to Allen Bird on a counter-option, the next play dump pass to Joe Kramer." I thought those two plays, one right after another, might just get us a first down.

"Okay, Coach," he said and ran to the huddle.

The hand-off to Allen went 60 yards for a touchdown. Ninilchik fumbled on the kick-off and before I could send in another play, Robert ran my second play.

It was too late, but I yelled, "No, don't throw a pass on first down!"

Robert threw a pass to Joe, and Joe ran for another touchdown. Boy, was I glad that Robert did exactly what I told him to do. That touchdown put us ahead by one point for good.

Soon wrestling season was upon us. We put a good team together and gained a lot of respect for Homer. We had a winning season and sent five people to the state tournament. One placed third.

One of those boys who went to state was George Raven, a transfer student. He was tall, lanky and strong, with that kind of wiry strength that comes from working on the farm all his life. Back in those "old days" a farm kid got his strength by participating in activities that can be duplicated in very few places. Often his father or some other authority would yell, "Get that hog." The young man would soon find himself wrapped around the hind leg of a 400-pound hog that was kicking with the ferocity of a jackhammer, but he dare not let loose or his dad might do worse to him. That kind of stress to the body makes one mighty tough very fast. George was that kind of tough. George wrestled well the entire season. There was never a young man with a better attitude or more mature outlook among all my wrestlers. It was a pleasure to have him on the team, and it was a pleasure to see him wrestle well enough to take second at regionals and go to state.

But George had had a rough life. He'd lived with his single mother most of his life and helped her scrape out a living. His mom finally married Bob Grimes, an old cowboy-type from Homer. It looked like things might turn around for George and his mother. They now had a "dad" who cared a lot for them and things were going to be a bit more stable. It's too bad it didn't turn out that way.

Bob Grimes, George's stepdad, was one of those people born out of time. He was a cowboy through and through. He walked bow-legged from riding horses, wore his old beat-up Stetson, talked in Western slang and had a look in his eye like he really wished he was out on the cattle drive instead of wherever he was. He owned a few horses and a few cows and believed in "open stock range," meaning if you had valuables you better fence them because he wasn't fencing his animals.

Now the rural law of Alaska was open stock range, but most of Bob's neighbors didn't understand. They just got mad at Bob when his cattle or horses got in their gardens. But Bob got along well, because he had a big heart and was always helpful to his neighbors when asked, although occasionally one of them called the cops about his animals.

Bob was poor as a church mouse himself, but he did have one prize possession: a registered quarterhorse stallion. He was a real beauty; black as the ace of spades, one small star on his forehead. For a quarterhorse he was big, but moved with that quarterhorse quickness. Bob always kept him curried and sleek as a pigeon, because this fine stud was a major source of Bob's income, meager as that was.

Then one day his quarterhorse stallion came up missing. He thought that one of the neighbors maybe tied it up, or worse, but as he asked around nobody had seen it. He hunted for several days when he heard a rumor that Cal Jesse had his horse. He went to Cal and asked for it, but Cal said he knew nothing about it. After a few more days of hunting, the rumors persisted that Cal Jesse had the stud. Bob went to the local police about it, but they ignored him. To the police, Bob was just that farmer everyone was always complaining about.

Another day went by and again several people told Bob that they had seen Cal Jesse with his horse. Bob decided to do what any cowboy would do and took matters into his own hands. He went over to where he knew Cal kept some of his horses, rounded them up, put them in a corral and sat outside with a gun demanding Cal bring him back his stud. Cal drove up with his son and two bigger guns. And so ensued "The Shootout at the Homer Corral." It might have been a funny incident, but Bob was killed and Cal's son was injured. Two days later the police caught Cal hauling Bob's stud down the road in his horse trailer. The horse was confiscated, but the police never filed any charges against Cal. I think it may have been because Bob was not a popular person with the police.

The end result of Bob's death was that George didn't stay in Homer and moved the next year back to the Lower 48, and he didn't get to wrestle for Homer the following year.

The wrestler who took third that year for Homer was Anders Togustad, a big blond boy of Norwegian ancestry. Anders looked every bit the fierce Viking of Norse history. It was easy to imagine that huge figure of a man standing at the head of a Norse ship, face covered with blond beard, wind blowing his blond locks, all crowned by his horned helmet.

He was one of the best wrestlers in the state that year and had improved so much during the final weeks of the season I was sure he'd win the state championship. But he lost his first match to a powerful-looking young black man named Harvey Lynn. What surprised me was that several times Anders had Lynn on his back, only to be suddenly turned to his own back. The final score was ridiculous: 28-27.

After the match I asked Anders what happened.

"Coach, I woke up with a cold this morning," Anders said. "I've been dizzy all day and I can't seem to even walk right."

We were able to get him to a doctor quickly. The doctor said the cold had invaded his inner ear and thus affected his balance. A few nose drops and Anders was back in business. He won all the rest of his matches and took home a third-place medal. I always wondered if, without the cold, he could have won it all. Harvey Lynn placed second in the tournament, losing to the champion by one point.

We had a lot of fun as well that year. One young man who was going to the local bible college came down every day and would wrestle with the team. He was a nice, clean-cut fellow, and a good influence on the kids. Bob Rhenium was his name. One day while we were all in the shower, soaping down after a hard practice, I asked, "Bob, what are you studying up at the bible college this year?"

"The Old Testament," he replied as he was washing off the thick soap.

"I have a philosophic question for an Old Testament scholar," I said. "Did Moses take turtles on the ark?"

"Moses took everything on the ark," he solemnly replied.

"No, he didn't," I returned. "It was Noah on the ark, not Moses."

The wrestlers just howled. Bob threw his hands to his head and said, "I can't believe I said that."

Chapter 20

Being a father is the most rewarding experience I can imagine. As a schoolteacher I've never been able to buy a lot with my salary, but I'm the richest man in town. I've always felt that I wouldn't trade any one of my seven children for a million dollars, and I'm sure no one in Homer, Alaska, has more than seven million dollars.

It is important to use psychology on children however, and if you're smart you can get them to do anything. I'd grown up taking a spoonful of cod liver oil every day. My wife hadn't and couldn't even stay in the same room with an open bottle. However, our three older children were constantly having runny noses in the cold Alaska winters and somewhat in the cold Alaska summers. Nina was talking to my mom on the phone about the problem and Mom mentioned her use of cod liver oil for the very purpose of runny noses. Nina decided to try it. She bought a bottle of the wretched-smelling stuff, but was wondering how she could get the kids to take it. Especially since she could not even stand to open the bottle.

"I'll take care of that," I assured her. The next morning, after breakfast, with all the excitement of a ringmaster at the circus, I said, "Children, today we get to take some cod liver oil. It's great!" And I spooned into my mouth a tablespoon of the fish oil. "Of course we only have one bottle of it, so there will only be enough for a couple days. Who wants to be first?"

"I do!" they all yelled in unison.

Cheerfully, each took their tablespoon of cod liver oil while my wife ran to the bathroom retching. Not once did I have trouble getting the children to take cod liver oil, and their runny noses cleared right up. In fact, one Sunday the kids were reluctantly eating their food. They hadn't had their daily dose of cold liver oil, so I said, "If you hurry real fast eating dinner, I'll give you some cod liver oil." To my wife's amazement they all dove into their food eagerly so they could line up for the cod liver oil.

Summer came again and I was able to get a local painting job so I didn't have to work away from the family. I was also asked to be in charge of my church's local youth group. We decided to play softball for the summer's activity.

We had a great time, but after several weeks I could see we needed a challenge just to keep the interest up. So I went to another church group and challenged them to a softball game. They agreed. I decided to make it a big game so I took out an ad in the local paper.

Challenge of the Religions. Baptists versus Mormons.
Softball at the Community Baseball Field, 7:00 p.m. Wednesday.
All are invited to cheer on their favorite.

Wednesday night came and when we pulled into the baseball field, the stands were full of spectators. You might have thought it was the Crusades or the Coliseum, depending on your point of view. What looked like might be a riot turned into a great softball game. Everyone — players, spectators and coaches — were downright Christian to each other. We had a wonderful game, but the home team (us) lost. Then, Christian Community Church wanted to get into the fun so they challenged us the next week. They came, but with not enough players, so we loaned them some of our scrubs and they still beat us. Next we played the Catholics and all those churches played each other.

Soon there was talk of starting a city softball league. They had an organizational meeting for the next summer and the city league softball has been a going thing since that time. However, to this day our team has not won a game.

Chapter 21

The wonderful thing about wrestling is that it is so humbling. Like no other sport, it isolates a person and pits him one on one for total physical dominance. And yet at the same time, the team is a crucial element. Wrestling is like chess in that it is one on one, with a good amount of mental competition, yet is unlike chess in that it has a physical side. Wrestling is unlike many so-called "individual sports" such as track and field, because in those sports several participate at once and few notice who comes in last. In wrestling, when a participant steps on the mat, it is "mano a mano," everyone knows who wins and who loses. Once you are out on the mat, no one can help you out. No one can pick up the slack if you decide to not give it your best. You also cannot blame it on someone else if things go bad. The reason you lost is never that "no one threw me the ball" or the guy on the other side of the line missed his assignment. Each wrestler must face up to his own loss. Each also can take credit for his own win. There is no thrill like winning when you and only you did it, without doubt.

Yet there is this fascinating element of the "wrestling team." Some coaches and wrestlers underestimate the importance of the team because wrestling is an individual sport. But the team is irreplaceable in importance in wresting for at least two reasons. One is the sparring. In boxing, a sport very similar to wrestling, sparring is somewhat dangerous, so individual exercise and training are stressed, and sparring is limited. Wrestling, on the other hand, is relatively safe when amateur rules are adhered to, therefore sparring need not be limited. Sparring in wrestling is fun and all the wrestlers who are in the best shape have done a lot of it. However, to spar one must have a number of sparring partners. It is usually best to have someone who is better than you, someone who is not quite as good as you, and someone who is just about as good as you to spar with for best progress. That means there must be a lot of people on the team to obtain maximum progress for each wrestler.

The second reason the team is so important is that intangible team spirit. It is impossible for me to count the number of times I have seen wrestlers do the impossible when they felt that their team members needed them and were pulling for them.

The most frustrating and yet the most fun part of wrestling I call the "fickle finger of fate factor." I once was told by an old-timer the most exciting race to watch was a dog race because you never knew what was going to happen. He said that dogs would do the darndest things — stop and relieve themselves, veer into the path of another dog, start a fight, join in a fight, chase something they weren't supposed to — you never knew what was going to happen. I think wrestlers are like those dogs. Not that they look like dogs (though some do). Not that they relieve themselves in the middle of a match (though some do). It's more that they are so unpredictable, and yet at the same time such great athletes.

One example was Josh Duvall. Josh had great potential, worked hard in practice, but could never win against a tough opponent. Then in one important tournament, he was seeded against a two-time state champion. Josh demolished him. He couldn't do anything wrong. From the first takedown to the last whistle, Josh used move after move to perfection. No matter what his great opponent did, Josh countered and totally foiled everything this state champion opponent did. Josh wrestled like an Olympic champion. I just knew this was the start of something great for Josh. He won 18-2, but he never was able to wrestle another match even close to that caliber in his career.

Another time, John Williams lost the state championship over a contact lens. John was an extremely focused wrestler. He concentrated so hard on his opponent that he tuned everything else out. The strategy worked for him. His senior year he was undefeated and wrestled in the state semifinals against an opponent from Fairbanks whom he had previously beaten by wide margins. During the match, John lost a contact lens. The match was stopped, but the lens was not found. John went on with the match, but the loss of the lens broke his concentration and as the "fickle finger of fate factor" would have it, that was enough for the Fairbanks boy to win. John had to settle for third place at state that year.

Coaches are also often touched by the "fickle finger of fate factor." In fact, I'm sure more often than anyone might guess. So did it come knocking at my door that third season.

Al Poindexter and I had agreed to "team-coach" the wrestling team. We'd be partners and decide together how to coach. We'd alternate each year as to who was officially called head coach. This year was Al's year to be head coach. I was also coaching the junior high and had talked with another junior high teacher, Eric Harris, to help me coach the junior high team.

Both teams were tip-top. The high school team had wrestled a dual match with Kenai and lost by a scant four points. In wrestling circles, that is a very close score. Kenai was ranked by the newspapers as the number one team in the state, and eventually went on to win the state tournament that year. We were a very good team.

Homer had three wrestlers who were potential state champs. First we had Adam Beasley, a farm boy, who was as strong and compact as a work horse. There was only one boy in the state who could challenge him, a young man from Kenai, Mike Windell. They each beat one another in very close scores. Our second candidate was John Weston, just a junior, who had perfected a Fireman's Carry that no one could stop. Only Kenny Ashcraft, another wrestler from Kenai, was close to John. And then there was Will Wyatt. No one was close to Will. He was the meanest, orneriest cowboy in the whole state. On Halloween he would dress up in a hangman's costume and look for the rich high school kids, the smart kids, or the student body officers and beat them up. He just liked to beat up people. He was that mean. He couldn't hurt anyone in wrestling legally, but he loved to dominate them.

On a wrestling trip to Anchorage, we wrestled East High School, a school of about 4,000 students. They had a returning state heavyweight champion who eventually won the state championship later that year. To that point he had not lost a match in two years.

This young man looked like he could win Mr. Universe. His black body rippled with muscles. When he took his shirt off, a bulging six-pack of abdominals rippled with every movement. His arms were the size of most men's legs. For warm-up, he would leap up and grab the support on the basketball backboard, drop one hand and do one-handed chin-ups. This incredible hulk had the ironic name of Carver Lamb. If I were him I'd have changed my name, but everyone knew who he was and no one wanted to wrestle Carver Lamb. At least no one but Will.

We didn't have a heavyweight and for some reason East didn't have a 190-pounder, Will's weight. So I asked Will, "Do you want to wrestle Carver?"

His cowboy grin split his face from ear to ear, "Yah." I figured that mean yes, so I entered him as a heavyweight.

The crowd just roared when Will and Carver were announced. And well they should have. Two gladiators had stepped on the mat: Carver with a typical "boxer sneer" on his face, an Atlas in black; Will, still grinning, a bit smaller, but every bit a Hercules, face to face.

The whistle blew and the brawl began. And brawl it was, but neither wrestler could gain the advantage. Sweat rolled off their bodies as each muscled, pushed and threw the other around the mat, but neither wrestler could gain the advantage. With 10 seconds left, Carver locked his hands around Will in an illegal technical violation, giving Will one point. The match ended. Will had done what no other wrestler in Alaska had done for the last two years, he had beat Carver Lamb.

Carver shook hands at the end of the match like a gentleman, then retreated to the locker room where with head, fists and feet he broke, bent and destroyed several lockers before someone stopped him. Will had shown who was the toughest kid in the state, but Will did find something tougher than him on the way back home that day — a moose.

Chapter 22

In Alaska, moose are quite frequently seen on the road system during winter months. The roads are cleared of the deep snow, making travel much easier for the moose, as well as for the cars. Unfortunately, both large objects (moose and cars) often meet with devastating results for the cars and sometimes for their drivers. Of course, the collisions don't do much good for the moose either. More than 500 moose are killed per year on the Alaska highway system. The state of Alaska keeps track of the road kills and posts signs in various places on the highways, tallying the number of moose killed each year.

On the road back to Homer that particular wrestling trip, we came upon the scene of one of those tragic accidents. A car had clipped the back legs of a cow moose who was lying on the ditch bank, suffering, in pain, apparently unable to move. We stopped to see if there was anything we could do to help. The fellow who had hit her had not been hurt, but didn't know what to do with the injured moose. I informed the man, apparently who was new to Alaska, that he should call the Alaska Department of Fish and Game. They would come right out and take care of the moose, in this instance probably kill it to put it out of its misery, and then butcher it to be given to a charity. He decided to drive to the next gas station and make the call.

In the meantime, the wrestlers had all piled out of the van. The groans and pitiful sounds that were coming from the moose tore at all of their heartstrings, even Will's. Will went to the back of the van and dug out a five-foot pipe. Heaven knows why it was there, but for some reason it was. It was about two inches in diameter and its sides were of solid quarter-inch steel.

"Coach, I'm gonna put that poor cow out of its misery. It ain't right the poor thing should suffer like that," Will said and stepped down the bank with his five-foot pipe. Now, back in those days, teachers were not so concerned with lawsuits and not letting kids do anything dangerous as we are now. Also, I knew that this was not really any different situation than Will faced every day out on his Alaska bush ranch, so I didn't say anything when Will strode toward the head of the moaning moose.

With the practiced swing of someone who had split a lot of firewood using all the force of his Herculean strength, Will connected that steel pipe to the top of the moose's skull. The pipe and Will's arms quivered with the impact. The woods rang with the sound of steel hitting bone. To Will's and our surprise the cow moose jumped up, shook her head and charged Will. All of us scurried like scared rabbits around and into the van, Will not a half-second behind us. After a couple lunges, the cow again fell and slid down the bank.

"I must not have hit her square," Will finally drawled. "Think I'll try again."

"I think you better not," I said. "I don't want anyone hurt." About that time the moose groaned her loudest.

"Coach, we can't let her suffer like that. Let me try it just once more. I'll be real careful," begged Will.

The whole team got into it on the moose's side, and after another groan or two, I relented. "Okay, but you better be careful."

This time, with a lot more caution, Will sneaked to her head. He positioned himself and like some giant forest king, lifted up his steel weapon, and crashed it onto the head of the helpless cow. I know if that blow had hit me it would've broken every bone in my body, but the moose jumped to its feet, waved its head, scattered all of us and almost caught Will before he leaped into the door of the van. The cow again collapsed and slid down the snowbank away from the road and continued her moans and groans.

Somehow, Will talked me into letting him try again. Again, Will stalked and pounded the moose, and again she jumped up and chased him to the van. This time the moose braced its broken leg against the snowbank and stood ready to attack anything that might show itself out of the van. As far as we could see, Will had had no effect on the health of the moose. We drove away, leaving her to her pain. I hope the Fish and Game fellows brought a big gun to put her out of her misery, because she wasn't going to get killed any other way.

Chapter 23

The junior high team was a team to be proud of as well. I could tell with some development and encouragement there was enough talent to make an eventual state champion team in high school. I got a break in the encouragement category when Kodiak called us and asked if we could come over for a junior high tournament. Kodiak was kind of an exotic place in Alaska, an isolated island accessible only by air or boat. They so much wanted us to come that they were willing to pay our airfare over. I said I had to check with the principal, but I thought we could. I checked with Mr. Loosely who informed me he had delegated all athletic questions to his new athletic director, Joe Campbell. I went to Joe, who said it seemed fine. I explained to him that Eric Harris, my assistant coach, would have to take them and coach them as the tournament was at the same time as the high school regional tournament which I had to attend. Joe didn't have a problem with that, so everything was set. I called Kodiak and said, "Count on us." Then I told the junior high team.

The junior high kids caught fire over the idea. They worked harder and couldn't stop talking about going to Kodiak. Practice picked up and good progress was made. The junior high wrestlers took second to Kenai in the borough tournament, but "going to Kodiak" was their real goal. Things were going great both for high school and junior high. Then the Fickle Finger of Fate Factor wagged its ugly form.

First it wagged at the high school. The state tournament was in Sitka, a picturesque town in southeast Alaska, also known as the panhandle. The panhandle consists mostly of mountainous coves and islands covered with large spruce rainforests. There are few roads in Southeast and none connected to anywhere else. The saying "you can't get there from here" is a reality if you have to depend on roadway transportation. The only realistic option for the wrestling teams was to fly in, a rather expensive proposition. Nevertheless, all school districts had budgeted to do it, except Anchorage.

The Anchorage region was allowed to send 48 wrestlers to the state tournament. This was twice as many as any other region, but of course Anchorage had more than twice as many students as any other region. But 48 kids for Anchorage seemed to the Anchorage principals to be too much, so the Anchorage principals met together and decided they would allow only 12 wrestlers to go from Anchorage — only the first-place wrestler in each weight class. The Anchorage wrestling coaches threw a fit and pointed out how much disadvantage the Anchorage teams would have by sending half as many wrestlers to state as any other region. The Anchorage principals then used their considerable influence over ASAA, Alaska State Athletic Association, to force every region to allow only first-place wrestlers to wrestle in the state tournament in Sitka.

Next the Factor wagged at the junior high. Mr. Campbell called me to his office two weeks before the junior high kids were to travel to Kodiak.

"I want you to take a survey of the parents of your junior high wrestlers before they go. I want to make sure the parents are behind this trip."

"Okay," I said, puzzled. "What's this all about?"

"One of the teachers came to me and felt the junior high wrestlers shouldn't go, and I asked some of the other teachers. They all thought it was too much of a trip."

"But they won't be missing any school," I explained, exasperated.

"I know, I know, they were just concerned."

"I've already talked to most of the parents. They're all for it," I said.

"Well, let's just get that in writing. Here, I've got a permission slip I would like you to have each parent sign. If they all sign, the kids can go, but if not, you'll have to cancel the trip."

"Joe, you don't want this trip, do you?"

"Well, frankly, no. I agree with these teachers. I think you should wait until kids get in high school for trips like this."

"But you send the junior high basketball team to Anchorage every year," I pointed out.

"But that's basketball, this is wrestling."

"What's the difference? Is one junior high kid better than another just because he plays basketball rather than wrestles? Joe, why didn't you say something about your objections a month ago?" I asked.

"Just get the papers signed," Joe said.

"Okay. No problem. I'll get it done this week."

All the parents signed the permission slips. Kodiak bought the plane tickets and sent them to us. We were all ready to go. The Tuesday before the Friday when Eric Harris was to take the junior high wrestlers to Kodiak, and Al and I were to go to regionals came. Joe called me into his office.

"Well, I've decided the junior high can go to Kodiak. But you have to take them. I won't let Eric."

"What? Why, may I ask? You know that Eric is every bit as responsible as I am. He is a teacher just like I am. What is the problem with him taking the kids over?"

"That's my decision. If you don't go, you'll have to cancel the trip to Kodiak."

"But you know I can't go. I have to go to regionals with the high school team."

"I guess you'll just have to cancel the trip. But it's your choice. You decide."

"That slimy scalawag," I said to myself as I walked out of Joe's office. "He wants to cancel the trip, but doesn't have the guts to do it himself. He wants me to cancel it so I'll look bad and he won't. Of all the oily, underhanded things to do. I can just tell he's going to go far as an administrator. He is such a weasel." I thought it over the whole day. It seemed the only honorable thing I could do was to call his bluff.

On Wednesday I told Joe, "I'm going to Kodiak. Al is going to need your help at regionals."

"What? You're not going to regionals?" Joe asked.

"No. Al is head coach this year and we've talked it over. We both feel that this trip for the junior high kids is important and I should go." We had talked it over. Al felt that if I called Joe's bluff and said I was going to Kodiak, he'd back down and let Eric take the junior high, especially if we put a little more pressure on him.

"Yah, I'm going to Kodiak, but Al will need your help with the kids at regionals. That's a big bunch of kids to take up to Kenai with just one guy. Do you think you could go up and help Al out?"

"Well, okay," Joe answered in kind of a daze. He was clearly confused as to what to do. I don't think he ever really recovered enough to back down and suggest that maybe it would be all right for Eric to take the junior high to Kodiak. So I went to Kodiak.

The day before we left for Kodiak, Mr. Loosely called me in his office and said, "Steve, I feel real bad about this situation. I think you have done a fine job here with the wrestling team, but when you delegate you have to stand behind those people's decision. I want you to know we will make sure that you get to go to state with the wrestlers who qualify, no matter what."

That made me feel much better. It turned out to be an empty promise however, through no fault of Mr. Loosely's.

That night I got the high school team together at practice and explained in detail what had happened. They all seemed pretty disappointed, but agreed that I was doing the right thing.

"Guys," I said, "you've worked the whole season; none of you are slackers. You've worked hard, you've learned everything I've taught you, you've done everything Coach Poindexter has asked of you, and you are in great shape. I can only ask that you do your best. The rest will fall into place." I thought it was a pretty good speech, but no speech can overcome the Fickle Finger of Fate Factor.

We flew into Kodiak on Friday. The junior high kids could not have done themselves more proud at the tournament. We had four champions, eight seconds and two thirds. Only one wrestler did not place and Bart Cannon of the Homer team was voted Outstanding Wrestler of the tourney. We, as a team, took second and brought home the nicest trophy the junior high school had ever received. They came home thinking they were champions. Eventually this team of junior high wrestlers won the state championship for Homer as a high school team four years later.

I could hardly wait to call Al and tell him the good news, and also find out how the high school boys had done.

"Steve, all of them lost. We had three seconds and several other place winners, but no champions," Al said over the phone.

"What about Adam?" I asked. "We moved him up a weight class away from Mike Wendall. He should have won that weight class."

"Kenai moved Mike Wendall up also to get away from Adam. They had to wrestle each other and Wendall won by one point."

"What about Weston?"

"He lost on a controversial referee's call by one point to Ashcraft," Al answered.

"But I can't believe Will Wyatt lost. Who beat him?"

"He wrestled terrible, and a Kodiak kid that he'd trounced before beat him by one point. It was the worst nightmare of my life. Joe Campbell went up with us, then sat in the stands the whole time. I had a kid injured on both mats at the same time and no one to help me. Steve, never do this to me again."

I was stunned. "So no one is going to state?"

"No one," replied Al. I was silent. I would never have believed a team could have such bad luck.

"How did you do in Kodiak?" Al asked.

"Oh, fine, fine," was all I could say. The Fickle Finger of Fate Factor had got us, but good.

Kenai won the state championship that year and the two Kenai boys, Ken Ashcraft and Mike Wendall, were state champions by large margins as well as the 190-pound boy who had beaten Will Wyatt. But what could you do when you've been gotten by the Factor? All you can do is shake it off and get in there hard the next time. Unfortunately, Adam and Will were both seniors and never got another chance. Adam, the rough tough farm boy, went on to graduate from college and became a fine artist and art teacher in the community. Will stayed mean. Several years later he was living in Anchorage; one night he was found shot to death in his parked car. Apparently he met someone who was meaner that he was. John Weston was a junior and had another year for his revenge.

Chapter 24

No matter how bad school and wrestling were, home made up for it. Our fifth wedding anniversary came and I asked Nina what she wanted for our anniversary.

She said, "A day off! I'd just like a day to sew or quilt or just be by myself."

"Well, our anniversary is on a Saturday. I'll take care of the kids and you can do what you want. That will be your anniversary present from me."

"No, you'll run off to some wrestling match."

"The season is over. I can spend the whole day at home."

"That will be nice. I think I'll go over to the church and quilt. I've been wanting to finish a quilt and there is lots of room there and it will be quiet."

Saturday came and all went well. I ran into town, got a cake mix and baked and frosted an anniversary cake. I had Ivan, Becky and little Nina all help as much as they could. Becky stirred, Ivan licked out the bowl when we were done, and Nina just cooed and kept us company. They were all excited about the "cake for Momma." I wanted to surprise her with the cake after dinner, but I knew she would smell it as soon as she walked in and I knew she'd look for it. So I needed a good hiding place. The kids suggested I hide the cake in the top of the closet, an excellent suggestion. "She'd never look there," I thought. Ivan and Rebekah were so excited they just couldn't wait for Mom to come home.

Nina did finally come home. She stepped in the house and said, "It smells like cake."

All three kids giggled.

"Don't look in the closet!" Ivan piped up.

So ended the surprise, but the cake was good. We ate it before dinner.

Chapter 25

Mom and Dad came up that spring "to do some fishing." They were able to fly up before the spring planting. Dad caught some salmon and halibut, but we couldn't keep him away from the farm. He had to see an Alaskan farm. So we walked out to Ed James' sheep ranch and met and talked farm talk with Ed. That's a nice thing about farmers. It seems no matter how busy they are, they can always stop what they are doing and talk to a visitor.

Dad and Ed got along so well that Dad decided to stay several days and help him shear sheep. I walked on home and left Dad out on the wilderness homestead to do his farming. Mom wasn't real happy that he'd stayed out there and, as a matter of fact, she had received a call that meant they had to go back early. I didn't want to walk all the way back, so we tried to call Ed on the CB radio.

CB radios at that time were the means of communication in Alaska. There were few telephones and those only in town. So for communication nearly everyone out of town had a CB. There were two problems with CBs: one, they weren't private. People kept their CBs on all the time. In fact, it was kind of the evening entertainment for some of those old homesteaders to listen to the conversations on the CB and to speculate and laugh and gossip about each. So you had to guard what you said.

Second, CBs were inconsistent. Some days you could hear and broadcast 200 miles away, and some days you couldn't reach the other side of the house. Well, it was one of those you-can't-reach-the-other-side-of-the-house days for our CB and we couldn't reach Ed. We tried 'til late when Nina told us to go to bed and she'd get a message to Dad so he would come down and catch the plane in the morning. Nina used our phone and called the city police who couldn't reach Dad on their more powerful CB, but they got ahold of someone who could get ahold of someone who could relay the message to Ed James.

The message did get to Ed, but it ended up like this (and of course it was broadcast all over CB land): "A message for Ed Wolfe from the Homer police. You are to get out of town tomorrow. Catch the 9:55 plane."

For weeks people were asking me how come my dad was kicked out of town.

Chapter 26

Somehow I volunteered or someone volunteered me to take the Alaska wrestling team to the national tournament in Iowa City, Iowa. I think it was at one of those meetings where if you don't show up they elect you president. Anyway, I was in charge of practicing with the wrestlers and coaching them at the high school national championships.

It was kind of an honor and actually turned out to be a fun trip. Rob McAuley from Chugiak placed second, putting Alaska on the wrestling map, so to speak. The University of Iowa was particularly nice to us and gave us the air-conditioned dorms to stay in. They were sure that Alaskans would melt without some cold air in the Midwest summer heat. They were probably right.

The most impressive thing for the Alaska wrestlers was the lightning storms. None had ever seen a lightning storm like the Midwest produces. Drenched, the whole team stood on the roof of the dorm, yelling to each other.

"Wow, look at that one!"

"Over there, look at that!"

"Wow!"

Perhaps the most noteworthy event was the change two boys from Kenai, Mike and Ashley, made. They changed their religion. And they did it even before they left Alaska.

We were to practice the week before we left at Chugiak High School in Anchorage. The Anchorage School District had a policy not to let anyone stay overnight in their facilities, so I had to make arrangements for those boys who were from out of town to have a place to stay the week we practiced. The Chugiak coach happened to be a Mormon bishop and volunteered the Mormon church to have the kids stay in, since no one would be using it the days we were there.

It turned out that Mike and Ashley were the only boys who needed the place to stay. Everyone else was staying with friends in Anchorage. I was going to stay at the church with Mike and Ash, to keep them under control, which is always a challenge with high school boys.

The first day after practice, I was ready to go when Mike and Ashley were still wrestling around.

"Let's go, guys," I said.

"We gotta shower."

"We gotta eat too," I said. "I'm hungry."

"We're not eating tonight. We both have to lose three pounds."

"Well, I'll tell you what. Pack up; I understand there is a shower at the church. I'll drop you off, you can shower there and I can go eat."

"Sounds good, Coach," they answered.

We drove over to the church. "I understand the shower is right next to the gym." I dropped the two off and went to a leisurely dinner. When I returned, Mike and Ash were just toweling off.

"Hi Coach," they greeted me. "Hey, Coach, we couldn't find the showers, but we found a big Jacuzzi and we took a bath."

"Jacuzzi?" I said. "Let me see this Jacuzzi." I had a big suspicion in my mind.

"Over here." They opened the curtain. I looked over the edge of the large tiled depression with stairs on each side.

"Guys," I said, "this is not a Jacuzzi. It's a baptismal font."

"A what?"

"A baptismal font. Where they baptize people," I answered.

"Oh, no!" they said.

"Oh, no is right," I returned. "What religion are you?"

"I'm Catholic," said Mike.

"I'm a Methodist," said Ashley.

"Not anymore," I said. "Now you are baptized Mormons."

"What? I can't be. I'm a Catholic," said Mike.

"My parents are going to kill me," said Ash.

"Sorry," I said. "Nothing we can do about it. Now you're Mormons," I gravely returned.

There was silence for a solid two minutes.

"You're kidding us, right Coach?" Ash asked rather tentatively.

I couldn't hold it anymore. I burst out laughing. "Yes, I'm kidding." They were both visibly relieved. "But we better leave this place cleaner than we found it. I doubt that the Mormons would appreciate us bathing in their baptismal font."

We showered at the school the rest of the week.

Chapter 27

Another year of teaching began and for the first time I was able to drive a vehicle to school. I had ridden a motorcycle to school the previous years. Well, it wasn't really a motorcycle; it was an old Honda 90 which is barely a step up from a bicycle with a motor. It was small. I rode it all winter, so I had this big, bulky, fluorescent orange snowsuit and a fire-engine-red helmet. I wanted to be seen by the other traffic. Most people in town said I looked like a bear on a tricycle. But it got me back and forth to school and left the car for Nina who had young children to take care of.

The old adage about not being able to see a motorcycle rider in traffic is true however. As I was driving my Honda 90 down the main street of town, a yellow VW bug pulled out of the post office right in front of me. There was nothing I could do but lay the motorcycle on its side and skid underneath the car. It was a main street, so my relatively low speed prevented much injury. But before I could stop myself I was up and had ripped open the VW door and was ready for revenge.

The driver slid over into the passenger seat, hands up to protect his face from my first swing, and said very sincerely, "I didn't see you, honest."

"How could you not see? Look at me!" I yelled.

"I don't know, but I didn't see you. Are you hurt?" He was so nice I knew he must've been telling the truth. So we got out of the car and surveyed the damage. It turned out to be minor to either vehicle. We each said we were sorry and went on our way. He was such a nice sincere guy that I was convinced that automobile drivers just don't see motorcyclists.

Anyway, that year I bought an old 1976 Datsun pickup. It had almost 100,000 miles on it and looked like it had been dragged through the muskeg once or twice too many times, but if you ignored the rust, the peeling orange paint and — oh, heck, there was nothing you could ignore. It was a bomb. But it ran great and in the middle of the Alaska winter it was a whole lot warmer than a Honda 90.

The first snow of the season had started as I pulled out of the school parking lot as usual. I was suddenly surprised as the road dropped out from under me and I crashed nose-first into a culvert. I was going so slowly I didn't get hurt, but the front of the pickup looked a whole lot worse. It obviously needed a new radiator and some other major adjustments to the front end.

Someone had changed the exit from the school to the state high-way. For drainage they had left a triangle-shaped area between the two exit roads which had never been there before. There were no markings on it and the drifting snow had filled it in so that it looked like one large exit-entrance area as there had been in the past.

After being towed to a garage and making my way home, I got on the phone. I called the city who said the state had done it. I called the state who said the borough had done it. I called the borough who said the city had done it. It took me several days to find that it was really the state that had done the construction. In the meantime seven more cars had driven right into the same triangle-shaped drain-age ditch. The local body and fender men were elated. The state still claimed it wasn't their fault, but did put some tripods with reflectors around the ditch. However, when I called back they would not admit that those tripods with "State of Alaska" painted on them were theirs.

It cost $1,500 to get the poor Datsun repaired. That was one month's wages. I didn't know how the kids were going to eat that month. So I called a lawyer. He listened to my problems and suggested I take the state to Small Claims Court. The amount I needed was so small it should be handled there. He also told me where I could get the papers and how to go through the procedure.

I filled out the papers, got on the agenda and went to court. A very sympathetic judge listened to my complaints and then said, "Un-doubtedly your cause is just, but you have to file a suit against the state in Superior Court. That usually takes months and your lawyer fees will easily be in the thousands."

I was just a tad embarrassed, but what really made my face go red was the next day when I got the bill for $45 from the lawyer with whom I'd spoken on the telephone. He charged me $45 for 10 min-utes of phone conversation and he gave me the wrong advice. I never liked lawyers much since then. Someone did tell me that if I went on state welfare for a couple months I could get my money back. I was tempted.

Chapter 28

When snow came, the hitchhikers came out. It seems all those people who wear mountaineer boots, who hike and ride bicycles all summer suddenly need a ride when it starts to snow. I have a lot of empathy for them. I had to hitchhike home from all my athletic practices during high school. Dad didn't mind me being in every sport so long as I got "my own way home." Hitchhiking was usually the way I got home. So as a semi-adult and owning a car, I picked up hitchhikers as long as they hadn't given up the hiking part of the hitching. I didn't have a whole lot of sympathy for those who sat on their sleeping bags at the side of the road with their thumbs up or holding a sign that said, "Timbuktu or Bust." The hitch-sitter I didn't pick up.

One day on the way home from school I picked up a hitchhiker. I happened to have Becky in the car. Her dark eyes got real wide, but she said nothing until I let the hitchhiker off. Then she said, "Who was he Daddy?"

" A hitchhiker," I replied and explained what hitchhiking was.

"Why is he hitchhiking?" she asked.

"Because he doesn't have a car."

"Doesn't he have a mommy?"

"Yes, he has a mommy," I said.

"How come his mommy wasn't hitchhiking with him?" she asked.

I looked in those big brown eyes of that little concerned face. I couldn't answer. I could only chuckle.

Snow brings winter and winter brings Alaska storms. This winter we had some particularly bad storms. Mr. Loosely would never cancel school no matter what the weather. One particular storm hit Homer like a sledgehammer. Forty mile-per-hour winds drifted the heavy snows, blocking all roads. Kids stood for hours in the blizzard waiting for the bus that never came, freezing hands and feet. But we had to make up a day if we canceled school, so we had school. Those of us who could, walked to school. We taught two or three students a class, but we didn't have to make up the day.

The day after the big storm, in the seventh-grade math class, we were discussing why school hadn't been cancelled. I explained to the kids that it was a matter of law.

"In Idaho, where I grew up, a storm like yesterday's would be considered an 'Act of God' according to Idaho law. Or in other words it wasn't anybody's fault. So you could cancel school and not have to make it up. However, in Alaska law, a storm like yesterday's is considered 'a way of life,' so we must live with it and so if we miss a day we have to make it up later."

Everyone seemed to understand. I knew I was helping them see the logic. Then Phyllis, one of the most attentive of the students, commented: "Gee, I could understand why the laws of Utah would be like that, but I didn't think the people of Idaho were that religious."

I realized how well I had communicated and spent the next 15 minutes trying to explain the situation a little better. I managed to make them think nobody in Idaho was religious before I hit on the solution to our discussion.

"Our math assignment today covers the meaning of variables...."

Chapter 29

I believe the funniest people in the world are wrestling coaches. They are so funny because, like other coaches, they take themselves so seriously, yet the next minute can laugh at themselves and at the crazy situation with reckless abandon. I bet wrestling coaches have the best sense of humor of any group of people anywhere.

Like the time Coach Bernie Saunders was visiting us at the Homer Winter Carnival Wrestling Tournament. He had a unique system for coaching his wrestlers. He had all his wrestling moves numbered like some football coaches number their plays. As the wrestler got into each particular situation, he would coach from the sidelines by yelling out the number of the wrestling move he was to use next.

This was a rather clever strategy because wrestling moves usually have rather standard names and when a coach yells out "half-nelson, half-nelson," his wrestler does know what to do, but the other wrestler knows what to counter and his coach knows what to yell back. (Of course, all of us experienced coaches know few of the wrestlers listen anyway.)

At this particular tournament, Coach Saunders was coaching his state champion wrestler against a much less-experienced wrestler. They were on their feet, wrestling for a takedown, and Saunders' wrestler should easily have taken his opponent down, but he was having trouble. During the whole first round Coach Saunders kept yelling, "Number three, number three, number three!"

The match went on and Coach Saunders' boy was finally called for stalling. At the break he crept over to the side of the mat as far as the referee would allow and said in just a little above a whisper, "Coach, I can't remember what number three is."

Coach Saunders just threw up his hands, turned around and laughed. I had to laugh with him.

Referees get their digs into the coaches quite frequently. What the coach sees and what the referee sees often seem to be quite different. Especially if the referee's call is to the disadvantage of that coach's wrestler. Once or twice this even happened to me. One particular time Fred Goldthorpe, a fine Alaska referee, called a takedown just as the wrestlers went out of bounds. Of course it was my wrestler taken down and I couldn't believe control had been given.

"Takedown? Takedown?" I yelled in total skepticism.

Fred said loud enough for the whole crowd to hear, "Yah, that's the way I saw it too, Coach."

He got me there. All I could do was laugh.

Coaches are the best at getting each other and Steele Jones was premiere in the pranks-on-other-coaches category. Steele was one of the old sourdough coaches. He had been coaching forever, a living legend as a wrestler and coach. In the off-season he ran sled dogs, trapped and chopped trees down just for the fun of it. He was tall, lanky, wore a big handlebar mustache and mountain man haircut. His guttural base voice could be heard all over the gym when he coached his Palmer wrestlers. He was a grand old man and he loved his practical jokes, especially on young inexperienced coaches.

This year there were about five fairly inexperienced coaches in the region. One weekend all region coaches were at a tournament and in the coaches room eating our usual fare of doughnuts and drinking pop. (Wrestling coaches are big on nutritious food.) Steele spoke up, "Hey, I see several of you coaches have guys with nosebleed problems. You know there's one surefire way to stop a nosebleed. It works every time and it works when nothing else will."

We were all ears. Nearly every coach had at least one wrestler who had nosebleed problems some time during the year. "What's that Steele?" I asked. He seemed pretty serious and he was such an old salt in wrestling circles that you listened when he spoke.

"Yah, it sounds funny, but if you take off their shoe and sock on their right foot, it has to be their right foot, and slap them on their bare feet with the bottom of the shoe, it stops the nosebleed cold. I don't know why it works. Must be one of those Chinese acupressure things, but it works. Take my word for it. It works."

Nobody argued with him. I just knew I was never going to slap my kids on the feet even if they bled a pint. Besides, I saw a little gleam in Steele's eye when he talked, even though he sounded dead serious and very convincing.

That next round a Palmer wrestler met a Wasilla wrestler. In the third round the Wasilla wrestler developed a nosebleed. The Wasilla coach whipped off his boy's shoe and sock, and started beating on his foot with the wrestling shoe. The wrestler screamed in pain. Blood ran all over his face and chest as the nose continued to bleed. It was several minutes before the Wasilla coach tried a more conventional method of stopping the nosebleed. I don't know if he ever saw Steele on the other side of the mat hee-hawing, rolling around on the mat and holding his sides. Steele laughed so hard he had big tears running down his cheeks. Boy, did that big mountain man love a good joke. Especially when it turned out so perfect.

Chapter 30

Bloody noses have been a perennial problem in wrestling. The strain that one puts on his body when competing one-on-one with an opponent is tremendous. One of the manifestations of that strain on some wrestlers is a bleeding nose. It is a harmless situation which is usually fixed by plugging the nose with cotton and continuing to wrestle.

This year I had two wrestlers, Phil and Bill Clawson, who ended up with nosebleeds every match. In fact, I could tell when they weren't really wrestling hard. Both boys got bloody noses when they really wrestled their best. They went to doctors who cauterized their noses, but that only lasted a couple weeks. So like most wrestling coaches, Al and I carried a pocketful of cotton to every match. The most efficient way to stop the bleeding was to plug the nose with cotton, which prevented the bleeding until the plug came out.

In these days of AIDS and other bloodborne-pathogen scares rampant throughout the world, no blood is tolerated in wrestling. If any shows, the match is halted, all bleeding is immediately contained, the blood is cleaned up and all surfaces are disinfected before wrestling continues. Back in those times, AIDS was unheard of and certainly not a threat to anyone in Alaska, so a little blood here and there was tolerated.

One particular time, Bill Clawson was wrestling a boy from Seward. I could tell he was wrestling hard because his nose started bleeding from both sides. We dutifully plugged it up. The match progressed and Bill turned his opponent over on his back. Now the real fight began. The young Seward man fought desperately to keep from being pinned; Bill just as intensively and intently was holding his opponent on his back, going for the pin. Bill was holding on with every muscle. He had buried his head in the Seward boy's chest to give him more control. The referee was on the mat looking for the pin and didn't see both cotton plugs come out ahead of a torrent of blood. Blood covered the Seward boy's chest. Bill continued to keep his head tight to the chest, so intense was his desire for the pin. Blood smeared over his entire face just as the referee yelled, "Fall!" and slapped the mat, signaling a pin.

In elation, Bill jumped to his feet, arms raised in triumph, and faced the crowd. Blood covered his entire face and colored it fire-engine red. He looked every bit like a blond Neanderthal who had just eaten the heart out of his live victim.

Chapter 31

"How old are you, Coach?" Russell Cates asked me.

I've never been ashamed of my age, so I promptly answered, "29."

"29? Coach, my mother looks younger than you and she's 39."

"Yah, but she uses make-up," I came back, and everyone laughed.

Getting old has never bothered me. I always felt that age was a sign of wisdom and demanded respect. However, my age as far as looks must have crept up on me pretty fast and it was Dad who indirectly pointed it out.

Al had an unfortunate accident and was injured with a Skil saw. He was laid up and unable to go with the team to a dual match in Chugiak. So I was up in Anchorage with 24 rangy high school boys by myself. I was really looking forward to the trip though, because Dad would be in Anchorage for a Northwest Farmers Convention. He didn't have much spare time, but he was going to come to the wrestling match. It would sure be good to see him again.

True to his farmer character, about the first thing he asked me was, "Can I help in any way?"

Boy, did I appreciate that offer. One coach running a JV and varsity team, preparing equipment, ferrying them to eating establishments between weigh-ins and wrestling was more than could realistically be handled. Dad pitched right in and helped wherever he was needed. He used his good-natured humor to keep the kids entertained and helped them get to their matches on time. I really appreciated his help and I believe the team did also.

We finished a good match and were just getting the kids showered when Dad said, "Steve, I've got to get back to the hotel."

"Let me walk you to your car." We chatted as we walked out in the parking lot. I told him how much I appreciated his help and tried my best to thank him.

"Steve," he said, "I'm afraid I might have embarrassed you and your team tonight."

"How's that?" All I could think of was how much help he'd been.

"Well, when the match was going on I went up and sat in the stands with the spectators. You know how excited I get at a wrestling match?"

"Yah," I said. I remembered how he used to come away from our high school matches complaining that his neck hurt. I'm sure it was from the fact that he wrestled every match we wrestled, only he did it up in the bleachers. A bridge would be rather a neck-straining move when done in the bleachers.

"Well, I kept yelling, 'Do a Princeton, do a Princeton,' " Dad continued. "This guy in the bleachers below me, real sarcastic-like, said, 'What's a Princeton?' Steve, I'm sorry, but I couldn't control myself. I said, 'This!' and stuck it on him right there in the bleachers."

"Dad, the Princeton is illegal now."

"It is?" he asked, somewhat perplexed.

"Yah, a couple years ago it was determined to be too painful so it was made illegal."

"Oh. Maybe that's why he screamed so loud. Anyway, I was never so embarrassed in my life after I did it, but ya know, heat of the battle and all that. I hope it didn't embarrass the team."

"No, Dad, I'm sure it didn't embarrass the team. If anyone even knew about it, they'd be proud they had such an enthusiastic fan."

"Well, Steve, I sure love you and I think you're doing a wonderful job with your team," Dad said as we shook hands goodbye.

"Have a good trip home and tell Mom I love her," I said.

"I will, I will," he said as he drove away.

When I came back to the locker room, all the team crowded around me. "Who was that, Coach?"

I realized I hadn't even introduced my father to the team. "My dad," I said, rather proudly.

"No way," Jim returned. "We all thought he was your brother."

"Yah," Mark put in. "We thought he was your younger brother."

Chapter 32

That fourth year was a rewarding year. Most importantly because our fourth child was born, a beautiful brown-eyed, brown-haired baby whose smile lit up the whole world. She seemed a promise of better times ahead. We named her Rainbow and a sparkling rainbow she has always been in our lives.

Coaching wrestling was rewarding as well. By this year we had a tradition of having a tough wrestling team and that meant respect by all our opponents. Homer was a small school, about one-third the size of most other schools we wrestled, about one-tenth the size of some Anchorage schools. Several schools learned not to treat us like a small school however.

The number-one rated school in the state that year was an Anchorage school, Chugiak. I really enjoyed wrestling them. Chugiak's Coach White was a fine coach and a good friend. He was slightly overweight and slightly balding, but no one ever noticed any negative attributes because of his big infectious smile. It was obvious that his kids loved him and would do anything for him, but somehow Homer always wrestled well against Chugiak. That year we had taken them to the wire before they pulled out a victory with their last two wrestlers.

The next day we went over to Dimond High School, also in Anchorage. When we got to Dimond, to our surprise Chugiak was there also. The Dimond coach had decided to pit us against their JVs because we were a "small school" and their varsity was wrestling Chugiak that night. The Chugiak wrestlers got a big kick out of the arrangements. "Forget their JVs, you can kill their varsity," they said to our wrestlers.

We pinned every Dimond wrestler that night. For the next 15 years Dimond never again put a JV wrestler against Homer.

The Clawson brothers were constant winners. They were twins, but not identical, which was great because they weren't in the same weight class. Lane Jones was one of the strongest, toughest 155-pound wrestlers in the state. A sophomore, Doug Scalzi, was a consistent winner. Russell Cates was a steady winner, but John Weston was a wrestler with a vengeance.

John had missed going to state the year before by not winning regionals. This year he was not going to let his goal of winning the state championship slip by him.

The one boy who had beat him was Kenny Ashcraft from Kenai.

Kenny Ashcraft had gone on to win the state tournament the previous year, and he was back this year, again wrestling for Kenai.

John decided to do everything right this year. He spent time outside of practice running on his own. He lived about three and a half miles from school and every morning, in snowstorm or good weather, John was jogging to school. He was also very fastidious about keeping his weight down. He would only eat enough to keep his strength up without gaining weight. Of course that meant he missed a lot of the things he loved to eat. One practice he came in with the most outrageous story, but somehow I believed it.

"Coach, you won't believe what happened," John said.

"I bet I can. Try me," I returned.

"Well, last night I had the greatest dream. I dreamed I fixed myself two sandwiches. They were just like I like them — lots of lunch meat, cheese, tomatoes, pickles, lettuce, mayonnaise, the works. They were the greatest sandwiches I'd ever eaten. Every bite was so good. I could feel the texture, taste the taste. I ate every crumb. I then finished them off with a can of Hawaiian Punch. It was the best Hawaiian Punch I'd ever had as well. Coach, it was the greatest dream. I woke up with the most satisfied feeling that I've had in a long time. It was a great dream."

"Well, I'm really glad for you, John. Sounds like it was a pretty good dream, but I don't think it's all that unusual for someone to have dreams about eating things, especially when you're a little hungry," I said.

"But Coach, when I went out to the kitchen there was a plate on the table with the leftover crumbs of a sandwich and an empty can of Hawaiian Punch, and now I'm three pounds overweight."

John had a good season. He had won every match except two. His first match of the season he had lost to Kenny Ashcraft again. Late in the season he had lost to a Bartlett varsity wrestler in an Anchorage tournament. All other matches had been decidedly John's. He never rested on his record. He learned everything that we taught him and continued to try new moves. Toward the end of the year, he developed a Fireman's Carry takedown.

The Fireman's Carry is devastating to opponents because it has such potential for not only getting the takedown, but also putting the opponent on his back to pick up near-fall points as well as a possible pin. The Fireman's Carry, however, is such a technical move it often takes years to develop to a point that it can be used on all opponents.

Toward the end of John's senior year, he got it down. He couldn't wait to use it on Ashcraft. He got his chance at a dual match with Kenai two weeks before the regional tournament.

At this dual meet, John caught Kenny Ashcraft in the first 10 seconds with his Fireman's and Ashcraft spent the whole first round fighting to keep from getting pinned. Fighting off one's back is perhaps the most exhausting activity in wrestling. From that point John used his superior conditioning to continue to harass Ashcraft until the match ended with John a clear winner.

The Kenai coach told me afterwards that the match was a fluke and Weston would never again be able to beat Ashcraft.

"We'll see in two weeks at regionals," was all that I replied.

Two weeks went by and Ashcraft was seeded first (because he was returning region and state champ). John was seeded second. Neither wrestler had a serious challenge until they met in the finals.

To me it is an awe-inspiring event to see two superbly conditioned wrestlers step out on the mat to begin the match of their lives. High school and college wrestlers, with the weight classes set up as they are, produce some of the best-conditioned and well-muscled athletes in the world. Much different from professional wrestling which often produces overweight, but talented, actors.

As the two young men walked to the mat, their physiques, set of their jaws and flint eyes, all told a story of dedication, hard work and determination. It was almost a shame one of them had to lose.

John, with his dark wavy hair and natural olive complexion, was shorter than his opponent who was blond and fair-complected. Muscularly, John looked stronger, but Ashcraft's longer stringy muscles were deceptively strong and limber.

The match began and a great match it was. Wrestling is the sport that symbolizes life in every way. It is as well-prepared man facing his fiercest challenge — another well-prepared man. "Mano a mano" the Italians say, and they were talking about none other than wrestling. You have friends, team members and family who have helped you prepare all they could. But now they are standing at the mat edge encouraging you, but you, the wrestler, must step out on that mat and face the enemy. You must do it alone. To lose is bitter disappointment, but to win is great satisfaction. No greater satisfaction can come than to know you have met the challenge, you have overcome, but you did it alone. You did it because of your own prowess, your own determination, your own preparation.

So these two faced each other across the mat. They occasionally looked at each other with respect in their eyes, but this did not lessen the determination that was there also.

The match began. Ashcraft had obviously practiced staying away from John's Fireman's Carry. John shot a Fireman's again and again. Ashcraft blocked each attempt and backed away, not allowing his arm to be trapped by John. John stayed calm. He switched to a single-leg takedown, which would have brought to the mat any lesser opponent, but not Ashcraft. This defending state champ used his long legs and arms to spread out and cover John for an effective cover. Move, countermove, move, countermove, almost the entire first round passed. Like a windmill the wrestlers fought each other around the mat, then Kenny made his mistake. To defend himself from another takedown attempt, he underhooked John's arm. John ducked his head under Ashcraft's underhooked arm, reached between his opponent's legs and threw him right to his shoulders. It was a perfectly executed Fireman's Carry. John held him on his back five seconds before Ashcraft escaped and the first round finished. Victory for John was well on its way. The score was 5-1 in John's favor.

Before the second round started, Ashcraft had to choose the defensive (down) position or the offensive (up) position. He chose down. John was eager to begin. He could smell victory and wanted to increase his lead. The whistle blew, Ashcraft stepped up and out using his long body to stretch John out. He then quickly turned outside and grabbed John's outside leg. This quick action, combined with John's eagerness, made John slip to his hip. Ashcraft quickly reached over and hooked John's arm, putting John on his back. The referee was right on top of the situation. He quickly signaled points for reversal and stared counting for near-fall. John twisted and turned to his belly, but the damage had been done. Ashcraft was now tied with Weston, 5-5.

At John's choice in the third round, he chose down also. Ken Ashcraft's specialty was the cross-body ride, a move that allowed the top wrestler to control very effectively the bottom man and keep him from escaping. The top man would grapevine with his own leg around the near side leg of his opponent. Then stretching his body across his opponent's, he would keep him down and at the same time watch for a mistake by the bottom man which he could easily take advantage of and put him on his back. There were two very painful, but legal, moves that the top man could force on an unaware opponent — the guillotine and the banana split. Both were pinning combinations.

John knew the danger of each, but try as he could he was not able to keep Ashcraft from grapevining the leg and putting on the cross-body. John bucked, he kicked like a mule, he fought, he crawled, but he couldn't shake the cross-body. He needed only one point to win. He kicked and bucked some more, he finally hooked an arm and rolled both himself and his opponent off the mat.

It was close to the end of the match. If John was going to win in regular time he needed to do something now. The wrestlers were again started in the center. The starting whistle blew. With tremendous effort, still in bottom position, John jumped to his feet, twisted, turned and faced Ashcraft, completely getting away and earning one point for an escape just as the horn ending the match sounded. He'd won! He was regional champ and he'd beaten the state champion to do it.

John raised his arms in triumph and then jumped into the air. He bounced all over the mat before the referee was finally able to get him to shake hands for the ending ceremony. He shook hands, then leaped across the mat and jumped into my arms, wrapped his legs around my waist, buried his head on my shoulder and said, "Coach, thanks for teaching me the Fireman's."

In a situation like this, a coach shares every emotion. It was hard for me to say anything in return. I don't think I've ever been given a more meaningful compliment than those few words by that high school student. I finally somehow said, "John, you did a great job, just a great job, but this is only regionals. We still have state. Enjoy the moment, then start getting ready for next week."

Chapter 33

Thursday of the following week dawned as a beautiful, clear, bright, sunshiny day. It was spring and all the snow was gone. Freshness was in the air, as well as a touch of the scent of thawing dog and moose droppings. Nothing could refresh the soul as much as a beautiful day like this. Homer is beautiful all the time, but on a sunny day there is nothing to compare it to. I gazed at the ocean not 200 yards from the school and its sparkling blueness with those dark mountains just the other side of the bay, and it made me sigh with rapture. I'd been living in Homer for five years and I was still awestruck at the beauty of this diamond by the sea.

We loaded up the school van that morning to go to state. Four boys had qualified: Lane Jones, Russell Cates, Doug Scalzi and John Weston. They were a fun group of kids and fine wrestlers. I had confidence in every one of them. All were seniors except sophomore Doug Scalzi.

It was such a nice day that no one said a discouraging word, except Lane. "I just can't believe Lorrain Rhoder won the Winter Carnival Queen."

Lorrain Rhoder was a tall, slim and well-proportioned blond who could have passed for a model anywhere in the world. She had quite easily won the Homer Winter Carnival Queen contest the previous week with her sparkling smile and gentle personality.

"Why can't you believe that Lorrain won?" I asked.

"Well, she's good-lookin' and everything," answered Lane, "but in the eighth grade she was mean. She used to throw me into the snowbank at school everyday just because she enjoyed doing it."

We all laughed. Lane was one of the biggest, stoutest wrestlers in the state. It was almost impossible to image that slim, delicate blond throwing Lane anywhere. Teenage bodies change dramatically in just a few years.

The road was dry, the weather was good and there were very few cars on the road as we drove the 250 miles up to Anchorage. I was driving my customary 55 miles per hour when Russell chided me. "Coach, why don't you go faster? There's no cops around."

"No, sir," I returned. "I signed a contract with the state of Alaska when I got my driver's license that I'd obey the traffic laws. I figure it's a matter of honesty that I keep the speed limit."

"Aw, come on Coach, you can go to 65. The cops don't stop you unless you're more than 10 miles per hour over the speed limit," John added.

"I don't know about that, but I do know if I went over the speed limit

10 miles per hour, some of you yahoos would use that as an excuse to go 40 or 50 miles per hour over the speed limit in your own cars."

"No, we won't, Coach, honest," they said in unison.

"Well, maybe not, but I'm still not driving over the speed limit." I said it with such conviction that they knew there was no arguing with me. "Besides, look guys, there's a cop up ahead."

Sure enough a white Alaska State Trooper car had just come into sight, approaching in the opposite lane. I glanced down. My speedometer was right on 55 mph where it was supposed to be. I smiled to myself. There is a lot of self-righteous satisfaction in getting caught doing the right thing, especially when you have just preached such a wonderful sermon.

I glanced in my rearview mirror as the patrol car went by and to my surprise his brake lights came on. He stopped and turned around. I wondered why he had done that, because as I looked at my speedometer it was steady on 55.

Soon the flashing lights came on. I couldn't believe he was pulling us over. I dutifully drove to the side of the road and stopped. "What's the matter, officer?" I asked, very perplexed.

"I clocked you at 63 in a 55 mile-per-hour zone," he said.

"What?" I returned. "I was going 55."

He looked back at me with the patient look of someone who had heard that one a thousand times.

"Honest," I said. "The kids were just trying to get me to go over the speed limit and I was giving them a lecture why you shouldn't do it." I looked at my wrestlers. All had big sneaky-looking grins. They knew the irony of the situation.

"Isn't that right guys?" I asked.

Not one of them said a word.

"Well, maybe your tires are oversized. Oversized tires will cause the speedometer to read low. You should get that checked. However, the driver is responsible to know his speed regardless of his speedometer. I'll have to write you out a ticket." He began writing out the ticket. "Could I see your driver's license?"

I began fumbling in my billfold for my license.

"You know that you have a rear taillight out, on the right," he continued.

"No, I sure didn't. This is a school van and I'm not responsible for its maintenance," I informed the officer as I handed him my license.

"It is the driver's responsibility to make sure his vehicle is maintained up to state standards. I'm afraid I will have to give you a ticket for that." The wrestlers in the back seat were having a hey-day.

"Coach, it sounds like you should have read that contract you signed with the state a little better," one of them said.

The trooper continued, "Did you realize that your driver's license is expired?"

"What? It can't be!"

There was total hee-hawing chaos now in the back seat.

"Guess I'll have to drive, Coach," Russell piped up between his guffaws. I looked at my license and it had expired in February, in the middle of the wrestling season, and I hadn't noticed.

"Well, how am I going to get these kids anywhere?" I asked in exasperation.

"It's all right if you keep driving, it's not considered an illegal license, just expired," the officer replied. That was a relief. I could just imagine us hitchhiking up the road to the state tournament.

"I will have to give you a ticket for having an expired license though," the patrolman continued. "But don't worry too much about it. The taillight and license are basically fix-it tickets. You just need to get them fixed, have them inspected and there is no fine. But the speeding ticket will be an $18 fine."

"Well, if I have oversized tires, why don't you just give me a fix-it ticket for that?" I gave it one more shot on talking him out of the speeding ticket, but he wouldn't budge.

"I'm afraid I can't do that." He handed me the tickets and let us go on our way, me in stunned silence, the kids still giggling. All the way to Anchorage, about every five miles, one of them would ask, "How fast are you going, Coach?" and they would start giggling all over again.

I never did have very good luck in talking cops out of tickets. Anyway, not like Dad. I remember one time when Dad was driving his old farm Jeep and was stopped by a state trooper down by his farm in Idaho. Idaho had just passed a law that all vehicles had to have a safety inspection sticker. The officer said, "Ed, you realize that the law now says you must have this vehicle inspected to be driving it on the roads?"

Dad looked at the old farm Jeep, looked at the officer and said, as serious as a farmer could, "I didn't vote for that law."

The officer burst out laughing and said, "Go on home, Ed. And get this Jeep inspected or don't drive it on the road." I don't think Dad ever did get a ticket and here I had three in one afternoon.

We made it to Anchorage with no further incidents, but to this day I don't know why that trooper stopped me for speeding. I had the Homer Police Department check out the speedometer. They said it was accurate and the tires were the right size. When I told my story to the judge, he suspended the fine, I think for good behavior or something, so I didn't lose any money on the deal. I still don't drive over the speed limit, but I've never given that sermon again.

Chapter 34

The seeding meeting for state was Thursday night. By right of the victor, Coach Black from Kenai represented our region in this meeting. He did a great job except at the 167-pound weight class. There he had a bit of a conflict of interest. His boy, Kenny Ashcraft, was a returning state champion, yet had been beat twice by John Weston and was only runner-up in regions. Ashcraft had been beaten twice, both times by John. John had been beaten twice, once by Ashcraft and once by Mitchell from Bartlett. Of course Ashcraft had beaten Mitchell twice. Everyone had beaten everyone. When the dickering and shouting settled down, Coach Black did a great job. He got his boy Ashcraft seeded first, with Mitchell seeded second and John, the regional champion, seeded third. That meant that John and Mitchell would have to wrestle each other before the finals and that Ashcraft would more than likely sail into the finals with little competition. There was just something about John that told me, however, that it didn't matter what the odds were, he was going to win it all.

The games began — if a wrestling tournament can be considered games. A state tournament in wrestling is a wild event. Five, sometimes six, mats are being wrestled on at the same time. The action never stops; as soon as one pair of wrestlers is off, another comes on the mat. Those who love a three-ring circus would get even more of a kick out of a state tournament.

Our boys, Lane, Russell and Doug, all lost in the first round. They went on to win a couple matches in the consolation rounds before being eliminated. Disappointing for seniors Lane and Russell, but very encouraging for sophomore Doug who was able to win a couple matches as a sophomore in the state tournament.

John, however, had the greatest tournament of his career. He struggled in his first match. His opponent kept him at bay for two rounds; then it all fell into place. The score was 1-0 when John hit three successive takedowns to widen the margin to 7 before he cradled his opponent and pinned his shoulders to the mat for the ultimate win.

John never looked back. His next opponent he dispatched in the second round and advanced to the semi-finals. His opponent was Brian Mitchell, the only other man in the state of Alaska who had beaten him.

Meanwhile, on the other side of the bracket, as expected, Ken Ashcraft had pinned every opponent including his semi-final opponent, and was sitting comfortably, waiting for the finals.

The semi-final matches are usually the most exciting matches of the tournament. Every wrestler knows if he wins this one he is in for the championship, so every wrestler pulls out the stops. They all throw their best stuff at their opponent and the results are exciting to watch.

John and Brian Mitchell were about the same height and build. Not tall, but not short, both displayed powerful arms and shoulders. Mitchell had a silky smoothness about him that made him deceptive to wrestle. Somehow it seemed when John had wrestled him before that no matter what he did to Mitchell, like a snake, Mitchell was able to squirm out of it.

Mitchell was a good wrestler. I was concerned about this match, but John looked confident and ready to go. John had been wrestling since the second grade for this tournament. He wanted to be high school state champion.

The first period started and Mitchell reached for John's head. John ducked under the arm, hooked it with his left arm, shot in deep between the legs and threw his opponent across his shoulder to the mat — a perfect Fireman's. You could see the surprise on Brian Mitchell's face. He'd never seen this move done so well. Using his natural flexibility, he swivelled his hips in the air to keep from going to his back. John rolled hard to the side of Mitchell's chest, forcing him closer to his back. Mitchell fought, turned, flipped, swivelled and was finally able to squirm so that he prevented the near-fall, but was not able to prevent the takedown. Without mercy, John immediately broke Mitchell down to the mat, hooked an arm and drove him over to his back with a bar arm. Squirming and kicking, Mitchell again was able to get out of trouble, but not before John had picked up three more points. John's relentless attack continued; Mitchell was constantly defending himself without opportunity to retreat and regroup. The matched ended a route: John Weston 11, Brian Mitchell 0. John was in the finals.

There is something to be said for having to wrestle tough competition in the preliminary rounds as John did. Quite often the wrestler who's had the hardest time getting into the finals is the winner of the finals. So it was with John. That final match against Ken Ashcraft was an extension of his match with Mitchell. It was obvious from the first whistle that John was ready and Ken was not. Ken fought hard, scored a few points, but there was no question who was champion. John's moves were smooth, articulated and unstoppable, and at the last whistle John jumped to his feet and bounced around the mat in joyous exuberance. Ken stayed at the center on one knee, head bowed.

John's dad ran out on the mat and John jumped in his arms. John's dad was a fisherman in Homer and John was his only son. It was a great moment in both their lives. It was a great moment for us coaches. The Ultimate Win, the state championship win, and we felt we shared in that great victory.

Later that evening John asked if he could go home with his folks. He and his dad were going to take a couple of days out on the boat, just being together and celebrating the victory. He probably wouldn't be at school Monday. Sometimes family times like this are more valuable than any schooling. So I said, "Fine." I'm doubly glad I did because a few months later, while cutting firewood, John's dad was killed in a freak accident. John was forced to take up the family fishing business, which he still does today. He is now a very successful fisherman and helps run the Popeye Wrestling Club, a program for elementary-age wrestlers in Homer.

Chapter 35

"Coach, when are we going to get football here?" This was the hundredth time I'd heard the same question. This time sophomore Doug Scalzi was asking. His father had played for Bear Bryant at Alabama.

"Shall I give you the answers the administration has given me?" I replied. "We don't have a field."

"But, Coach, you know we do. The town rugby team plays on it every year and they even welded up some good goal posts."

"The weather is too bad here."

"Coach, why are you saying that? You know as well as I do they have football at Kenai, and in the high schools in Anchorage and Fairbanks, and the weather there is worse than here."

"I know, I know. I'm just repeating the excuses they give me. It costs too much."

"Coach, the borough pays for Kenai's football. Why can't they pay for ours?"

Doug had all the correct questions and the correct answers. I'd asked them too, because high school boys had asked me about football. The answers that administration gave me were not valid. I knew it and somehow I felt that the administrators knew it.

"The only way you'll get football at this school is if there are a bunch of parents who want it and go to the school board and ask," I said. "And that will take some organization. The school board meets in Soldotna 80 miles away."

"Then we'll do it," Doug said with determination. And he did. With his parents' help he organized a big group of parents who wanted to see their kids have the opportunity to play football. They got on the agenda and made the trip to the borough school board. The school board listened to the request and voted to provide the money for coaching and equipment with the stipulation that the local advisory board in Homer approved.

The chairman of the advisory board I knew well. He grew up in Homer and had gone to high school there. He had nothing to do with athletics and had plainly told me he felt that football was barbaric and unhealthy, but he promised to be fair at the meeting.

The night of the advisory board meeting came. Usually about four or five spectators come to an advisory board meeting; this night the room was packed. There must have been 275 people in the room. There were not enough chairs, so most of the people leaned against

116

walls, chairs and desks. Burt, the chairman, called the meeting to order and got right to the business of football.

"We want to be fair to everyone here, so I'll first take a pro-football (no pun intended) comment, then a con-football comment." He proceeded in this order until there was no one left to speak against football. Then he said, "Well, I believe that's enough comments. We will go into executive session now to make our decision."

"Hey, wait a minute! I drove 20 miles across breakup roads to speak and now I can't?" yelled Stanley Smith.

"Sorry, we just don't have time to hear everyone," Burt answered. It was obvious that about 100 people had not got to comment. It appeared also that they were all pro-football.

Not too many people get beaten up in Homer, but Burt came close to it that night. Somehow he escaped into executive session with his life, followed by several yelling complainers. Executive session was held and surprisingly, the decision was made not to support football.

"Why Burt? Why did the board vote against football?" I asked Burt later that evening. I was just a bit miffed at the unfair way he had handled the situation, but somehow I kept my cool and remained calm enough to discuss it with him.

"The expense," he said. "We just didn't want to commit to having the borough spend that much money for football."

"So if it was a club so that it didn't cost the school any money, the board would not be against it?" I asked.

"No one would be against it then," he replied.

I made no further comment, but made up my mind at that moment that it was time to stop talking and start doing. I did some phone calling the next few days and then called a meeting at lunchtime for all the boys in high school who were interested in football.

"We're going to have football next year," I stated.

"What? They voted against it," Doug answered.

"Yes, they did," I said. "But I had a talk with the chairman of the advisory board. He said no one would mind if it were a club, not sponsored by the school. I've done some checking and ASAA, the state guys who make all the rules, say we can play any high school team if we are a club. I checked on the insurance and insurance is actually cheaper if you are a club."

"Where are we going to get equipment?" another kid asked.

"I don't know that, but I'm going to write to some colleges and see if they might send us some of their throw-away stuff that we can fix up. The Elks have said they'd buy uniforms for us."

"This is great," Doug said. "How can we help?"

"Tell your friends and parents and plan on playing in the fall." And the meeting ended.

No one in the school, except me and the guys who really wanted to play, seriously believed that there would be football. Before school ended I went to work and wrote letters to every big-name football school in the northwest and to all the high schools in the state which had football, asking for donations. Within weeks equipment started pouring in. The high schools were especially helpful with helmets. A lot of them were changing from strap-suspension helmets to air-suspension helmets and they sent us all their strap-suspension helmets. Soon I had a garage full of football equipment, much to the chagrin of my wife.

One day I got a call. It was Coach Darrell White from Chugiak. "I'm down here in Homer repairing the wrestling mats and my football coach sent you some equipment."

"I'll be right over to get it. Where are you?"

"I'm parked in the parking lot right next to the gym."

"Great, I'll be right in."

It turned out he had his whole family down for the week while he repaired the wrestling mats. Later I brought my wife in to meet his wife and we chatted.

"Why don't you guys come out for dinner? We'll cook a few hamburgers and hot dogs on the grill, and Darrell and I can talk wrestling and genealogy," I said. It may sound unusual for a wrestling coach to have a hobby like genealogy, but both Darrell and I did. So it was doubly fun to get together.

"Have your kids had the chickenpox?" Nina asked. "We have a child with chickenpox."

Both Darrell and Linda looked surprised. "No, our kids haven't had chickenpox, have they?" Linda said.

"Well, it's about time they got exposed," Darrell said and we all laughed. "They're gonna have to get it sometime. We'll be out."

So they came over to our house and we had a great time talking over the wrestling season. Darrell had an 105-pound wrestler who placed second in the state, but to do it he had to shave his head to be light enough to make weight and wrestle the last day at state. He was a standout with his bald head among all those high school boys, especially during those years. This was the early '80s when everyone's hair was long and bushy. Darrell's kids got along great with our kids. They ran around looking under rocks for bugs, played tag and got in water fights. All in all we had a great time together.

Two weeks later, I got another call.

"Steve, this is Darrell. Just wanted you to know every one of our kids are down with the chickenpox."

118

Chapter 36

Earlier that spring Chad Chap, president of the United States Wrestling Federation of Alaska, called me. "Steve," he said. "What do you think of us hosting a regional Olympic trials in Alaska?"

"That would be great," I said. "Can we do it?"

"Yes. I've already checked with the National Olympic Committee. They said 'go for it.' But I need you and your wife's help. I need your experience in running a big tournament."

"Would that keep me from wrestling in the tournament?" I asked.

"I don't think so. I want to wrestle in it as well."

"That sounds real good to me. I'd love to help out. I'll have to check with Nina, but I think she will help out." Nina was the real brains behind any tournament we'd ever put on, but I thought she might look forward to a trip to Anchorage.

"Well, then it's on for late May. I'll get you some more information. I think I can promote it pretty big. What I'd like to do is raise enough money so we could send the qualifiers from Alaska to nationals," Chad continued.

"What a great idea," I said. "I'd be glad to buy into that."

We continued to communicate the next several months and Chad put together a great tournament. Service High School was rented, permission to have a regional Olympic trials tournament was obtained, and Chad promoted it through an Anchorage radio station and the local Burger Kings. There were contests for tickets and the enthusiasm caught on. Soon everyone was talking about the Olympic wrestling trials in Alaska. Many wrestlers from the northwest, Hawaii, Nevada and, of course, all the Alaska favorites, signed up to wrestle.

I dieted and got down to my old college weight. So did Chad and so did Steele Jones. All seemed to be going well. The money from spectator attendance and wrestler entrance fees would pay expenses, with about half of it left over for the Alaska wrestling team.

We had a great crowd; the stands were full. We had every Alaska wrestler, high school and otherwise, trying out for the Olympic team. The competition was fierce. The top two spots for most weight classes that qualified for the national tournament were taken up by out-of-state wrestlers, but Alaska had a few winners. Chad placed first at 136.5 pounds, Steele Jones first at 180.5 pounds and I picked up first at 163. We were all excited about going to nationals.

It seems that just when you think you have everything all figured out, and start patting yourself on the back, something in life lets you know that you are not really as smart as you think. This was one of those times.

We were cleaning up and counting the money when it happened. We first found that someone had broken into the locker containing all the wrestlers' entrance fees. That set us back quite a bit. But we still had enough money to cover expenses and a little bit left over. Then the second thing happened. Three guys and a woman showed up. They were rather hard-looking types, burly in the chest, and kinda looked Italian. I thought the Alaska mafia had come for their cut. But they informed us that they were from the Alaska AAU and had come to collect the wrestlers' entrance fees.

I was glad that there was more than just me standing there telling them to take a hike. They were rather insistent. I thought again of the mafia. They informed us in their New York accents that according to their charter, they were entitled to all entrance fees from Olympic trials. They suggested with the calm assurance of hit men that we really should call the National Olympic Committee and see if they were indeed entitled to the money.

At that time in the U.S. there was a fight over who was truly the national organization in charge of international wrestling — the United States Wrestling Federation or the Amateur Athletic Union. The AAU was winning out politically at the national level, but in Alaska the USWF was the only organization that worked with wrestling outside of high school.

We did call, and were told that, yes indeed, we must turn over the entrance fees to them. Chad and I were just a bit upset. The AAU had not offered or done anything to help with this tournament, and in fact their whole focus in the state of Alaska had been in the sport of skiing. And now they were showing up to collect the wrestlers' money. Something told us not to argue about it however. Something about these people also made us think that they would not believe us when we told them the money had been stolen. All we could think of was concrete boots, so we paid them with the money we had raised through gate receipts.

Now we had almost enough money for expenses. I ended up paying for the tournament individual medals, and Chad spent at least as much to cover other expenses, but we made it through the Olympic trials with our lives. And the money we gave the AAU we think was used to send Alaska skiers to the national skiing championships the following winter.

Chapter 37

"I've arranged for insurance that will cost the kids $25 each. The Elks Club has already bought uniforms. Several colleges and Alaska high schools have sent equipment. We have a schedule of games with Kenai JVs twice, two with Anchorage JV teams and finally a varsity game against Wasilla in October," I reported. I had called the meeting for those in the community who would be interested in coaching the club football team. Three showed up: Eric Harris, Brian Olson and Henry Pack.

"I thought we were meeting to organize the club for some future time. I didn't realize that we were ready to go," Henry commented.

"Neither did I," echoed Brian and Eric.

We then got down to seriously discussing who was going to coach what. Henry admitted he was going to be too busy to coach regularly this year. Eric and I felt that if either of us were head coaches, it might look bad inasmuch as both of us were teachers and this was not a school-sponsored sport. We felt that we could help as assistant coaches, however. That left Brian as head coach. Fortunately he had coached high school football several years before and was able to function in that position. It turned out that it was a good decision on our part.

Mr. Loosely, our principal, was beset with the plague that all good principals endure. If you do a good job as principal, you get promoted to the central office, where you can't do anybody any good any more. So this year Mr. Loosely was gone and we had a new principal, Mr. Linn.

Mr. Linn came with a reputation for being a no-nonsense, clean-up-the-place man. And he was tough. My first interview with him went like this:

"What's this about football?" he asked.

I explained to him that it was a club, that I was an assistant coach and doing it on my free time after school.

"Okay," he said cautiously. "But I'll be watching you very carefully. And when wrestling season comes, I'll be watching you very carefully also. I've heard about you," he said as he pointed and shook his long bony finger at me. "You had better behave yourself respectably."

"What do you mean by that?" I said, surprised.

"I mean, I've heard that you are a hothead and that you don't control yourself at wrestling matches," he returned.

"I don't know what you mean," I said. "I'm loud, but I've never lost my temper at a match. Who is telling you this?"

"Never mind that. Just remember I'll be watching you very closely this year."

When I was a kid, I was like most kids and hated to walk by the principal's office. I was always scared he might call me in and it was never for a nice chat about the weather. The next six months I re-lived that dread. Every time I walked by Mr. Linn's office I almost tip-toed. His long, tall, Ichabod Crane frame would be hunched over his desk and almost invariably if he caught my eye he'd crook that long finger at me, which meant again we were not going to discuss the weather.

Mr. Linn was actually a very handsome man in his long frame. He dressed like the 400 Club, but he never smiled and he never said one good word to me for the next six months.

"We had a group of citizens in here today who wanted to know why we had football when the advisory school board said 'no' last year. I told them it was a club, but, Wolfe, I'm going to be watching you very carefully, because I've heard about you...."

Later: "Wolfe, today the radio station was in here asking why I was allowing you teachers to coach football on school time. Are you coaching football on school time?"

"No," I said. "We coach junior high flag football on school time, but that has been a school-sponsored activity for five years. We don't start coaching the club until 4 p.m. and that is half an hour after all teachers are off-duty."

"Well, I'm keeping my eye on you because I heard about you...." And he lectured me about the wrestling season again as he shook his long bony finger at me.

Another time: "Wolfe, there were a couple teachers in here that didn't think it was right that you named your football club Mariners since that is the high school mascot."

"First of all, it's not 'my' football club," I countered. "And second of all, I'm sorry they feel that way, but it is a club and not sponsored by the school, so I think they can name it anything they darn well please. There's a Little League baseball team in town that has nothing to do with the high school and it's called the Mariners."

"Well, okay, but I'll be watching very closely. I've heard about you and...."

I could only mentally roll my eyes and endure.

Meanwhile, we were coaching football. If ever a more ragtag group of misfits put on football helmets, the world must have taken notice. We didn't have practice pants, so the players taped knee pads and thigh pads to their sweat pants, wore their hip pads strapped on the outside and pulled t-shirts, sweatshirts, whatever they could, over their shoulder pads. In practice there was no uniformity. They looked like refugees from a Salvation Army garage sale.

None of them except Doug Scalzi knew anything about football, except what they'd seen on TV. Running was poor, tackling was worse and blocking was nonexistent, but what they lacked in skill they made up for in enthusiasm. Rarely did any of the young men miss a practice. They listened hungrily to everything we coaches had to say, and then did everything in their power to make it work.

Every day in the rain, the mud or whatever, these kids eagerly came to practice so they could be football players. They knew so little about football that during the entire season if the coaches yelled, on a change of position, "DEFENSE!" the players would run up to the coaches and ask, "Coach, is defense when we have the ball or when we don't?"

Amazingly, this ragtag group was successful in winning a few games. The first game was with the Kenai JV team. Kenai had a fairly experienced JV team with a very fast runner. Our kids' experience was limited to watching football on television, but we played the game. They had to get experience some way.

Kenai got the ball first and the first play of the game they handed off to their fast runner. On the snap of the ball the Homer boys stood straight up and watched as the Kenai runner ran 80 yards untouched for a touchdown. I thought, "This is going to be a long season" and called a time-out.

I walked out on the field since I was in charge of defense. They all huddled around me. "Wasn't that great, Coach? What a great run," one kid said.

Another said, 'Yeah, that was just like the pros."

And another said, "This is great, we're actually playing football, just like Notre Dame."

"Yep, guys," I said. "It's great all right. The other team just ran 80 yards for a touchdown against you. You're supposed to try and tackle them. We're not home in our armchairs anymore. This is the real thing. We're not in Oz. We're back in Kansas. You remember us telling you about tackling?"

"Yes, Coach," they chanted.

"You know. Tackling. That's when you knock down the guy with the ball."

"Yes, Coach."

"Okay, now do you think you can play the game as well as you watch it?"

"Yes, Coach."

"Good, now let's PLAY some football."

"Right on, Coach."

It wasn't exactly a great pep talk, but play they did. The final score was 8-6 in Homer's favor. Kenai never scored again and in the closing seconds of the game Homer was driving for another score. The team went on to play four other JV games and won each by comfortable margins. But only one team, Wasilla, a new school in the Matanuska Valley, would play us a varsity game and then only late in October when their regular season was over. That game was a season in itself.

Chapter 38

"What's wrong, Warren?" I said. We were practicing in a new area where the grass had just been cut and cut rather long, but it was a fresh area, no mud. We were very happy to have a relatively clean place to practice. However, Warren Haws had just fallen down attempting to catch a pass. He had gotten up all right, but he was bent over gagging and apparently unable to talk or breathe.

Just the previous week I had read in the *Athletic Journal* about choking and a new technique to relieve it called Heimlich Maneuver. The article described how to do it, but I'd never tried it. However, this was obviously the time to try. Warren could not breathe, could not say anything. I moved quickly behind him, placed my fist below his sternum, just as the article explained, and with a quick in-and-upward motion of both my arms, pulled hard. Warren expiated a large gasp and immediately began breathing.

When he got his breath he asked, "What did you do, Coach?" I explained the new maneuver as if I'd been doing it for years.

"Coach, you saved my life. I knew I was going to die. I had a piece of grass caught in my throat and something in there would not let me breathe. I was just about ready to pass out when you squeezed and that piece of grass came out like it was shot from a cannon."

"Are you all right now?" I asked.

"Sure, I'm fine."

"Then, let's get back to practice." I don't think anyone else in practice even noticed what went on. Sometimes it doesn't take a large object to make you choke. A small sticky piece of grass lodging in just the right place will kick in the epiglottis valve (a small flap of skin that covers your bronchial tubes so you don't "swallow down the wrong pipe") and can prevent you from breathing as well.

Now the Heimlich Maneuver is a regular part of first aid curriculum, but in those days pounding the person on the back was thought to be the best technique for choking. That would have helped Warren out about as much as a shot of penicillin. To this day I'm grateful to Heimlich, whoever he is, and that article in the *Athletic Journal* and I bet Warren is too.

Chapter 39

It was the last football game of the year. As we drove the 300 miles to Wasilla, we began to realize that the mixed snow and rain we'd been having all week in Homer was all snow up this far north. When we stepped inside the stadium to look at the football field, we saw one full foot of snow everywhere. Any effort to plow it off had been left somewhere in the Lower 48 states. Instead of plowing the field, the custodian had taken advantage of all the snow and used a snow-blower to mark the lines on the field. For this game we had a white field and rather wide green lines.

"Good thing we had all those high-knee running drills," Doug Scalzi said. And he was right. To run through a foot of snow took exceptional high-step running. However, as it was during this game, running ability was not a factor.

It is hard to describe this football game. The snow was at its slickest and stickiest. All the boys' cleats filled up with snow and no one could stand up, let alone run. It was as if they had on hard leather soles and were playing on ice. One boy said he'd seen a professional game where a team switched to tennis shoes to play in the snow, so we all switched to tennis shoes during a time-out. It made no difference; still no one could walk, run or even stand up.

Besides not being able to stand, no one could hold onto the ball. Possession of the ball must've changed at least 75 times. Every play, the ball squirted out somewhere and hit the ground with 22 players all crawling, swimming or clawing to get it. The game looked less like a football game and more like those greased-pig contests at the rodeo. There was lots of scrambling and very little catching. The "ol' pigskin" had a mind of its own. It squirted out of every pair of hands that tried to hold it, and when on the ground, players scrambled, fought for it and only occasionally were able to hold onto it or trap it against the ground.

With all the diving, scrambling and chaos during the whole game, amazingly there were no injuries. The snow was so soft it cushioned every fall, and the ground so slick that no one could get up any significant speed, so nobody was hurt. A few fingers and toes got pretty cold, but no injuries.

We coaches were standing on the sidelines feeling pretty useless and frustrated until we noticed how much fun the kids were having. They truly loved the chaos. Every play was finished with a giggle, laugh or guffaw from every player. Finally, Coach Olson called a time-out and said, "Guys, just go out and have fun. Lord knows who is going to win this one and winning here proves nothing."

Wasilla won. They pitched out to a runner who somehow managed to get up some speed when everyone else fell down and crossed the goal line for a touchdown. It was the only play that went for more than three yards, but the kids came off the field at game's end saying, "This is the most fun I've ever had."

When I think about the emphasis we often put on winning in our modern society, I remember that snowy game in Wasilla and how much fun the kids had even though they lost by that one lucky play. And I say, "Doggone it, why couldn't we have been the ones with the lucky play?"

Chapter 40

"Daddy, do Eskimos really kiss by rubbing noses?" Becky asked me, her big brown eyes serious and concerned.

"Yes, I think they do," I replied.

Suddenly her eyes twinkled and she giggled. "That's not how Charlie Anafognak kissed me."

"What are you doing kissing Charlie?!" I said. It sounded to me like I was going to have to have a talk about kissing with our Eskimo neighbor.

"But Dad, Nina kisses boys at school all the time."

"No, I don't," said Nina Ellen. "I was just looking at their one-big-eye."

"What's that?" I asked.

"Well," said Nina Ellen, "you put your forehead against their forehead and touch noses, and instead of two eyes, you see one big eye."

"Oh, I've never done that."

"Let me show you, Dad." Nina and I put our foreheads together and sure enough all you can see is one big eye. Life with little children is very educational.

Rebekah was with us at her first-grade orientation and as the teacher was making her presentation. She took a poll at first and asked us to raise our hands if we lived in town, or out of town, if we had a telephone, and several other pertinent questions. Later on in her presentation she asked the rhetorical question, "How many of you love your children?"

Becky immediately said to us," Raise your hand, Mommy! Raise your hand, Daddy!"

Nina Ellen, who was just a year younger than Rebekah, was also fond of speaking out in a group. She had such a clear voice it was very easy to understand for one so young. As a family we went to the local show house, the Family Theater, and watched *Benji*, a movie about a dog appropriately named Benji. The movie had a suspenseful moment where everyone was calling out, trying to find the cute little dog. They were saying, "B-E-N-J-I, B-E-N-J-I." Then there was a pause in the movie and everyone in the theater was quiet, until Nina Ellen's clear little-girl voice from the back of the theater called out, "B-E-N-J-I, B-E-N-J-I!" Everyone heard it and the sweet humor of the situation incited laughter in the entire theater. Nina Ellen later became a cheerleader in high school. She probably doesn't remember that at the age of five she was already launched into her high school activity.

All parents are entitled to one "big" mistake when raising their children. I remember the big mistake my parents made on us boys. We were living on the farm and my mom discovered that we had pinworms. Being somewhat of a city girl, she was appalled and wanted to get rid of them immediately. Our grandmother had told Dad how to do it: Put a couple drops of turpentine in a spoonful of sugar and give it to the boys. That will take care of the worms. Dad thought he understood, but the cure was too close to the cure for worms in hogs. With hogs you mix a little turpentine with lard and feed it to them. Somehow Dad got the two cures mixed up. I'm not sure whether he fed the hogs turpentine and sugar, but he forced us to eat a tablespoon of lard and turpentine. I guess we were walking around for days gagging. But we never had any worms after that.

Our big mistake was with Santa Claus. Being new parents and knowing we had the world and especially raising children all figured out, we had ideals. One of our ideals was that we would always tell our children the truth and never deceive them, and then they would always be totally honest with us. So when the subject of Santa Claus came up, we were totally honest with Ivan and told him that Santa Claus was "make-believe" and that it was the parents who actually put the presents under the tree. We emphasized other aspects of the holiday and in no way did the non-belief in Santa Clause detract from Ivan's excitement about the Christmas season. Then he went to school and the subject of Santa Claus came up. Of course, Ivan blurted out the fact that Santa Claus was make-believe. What a stir it caused in the whole elementary school! Kids were crying and utterly dejected that Santa Claus wasn't real. It also made Ivan the least popular kid in school. Ivan went to Homer schools for 12 years and even during his senior year in high school he was known as the kid who killed Santa Claus.

Chapter 41

Wrestling season started again this year. The first day of practice pretty well indicated to me what kind of a team we'd probably have. I had two experienced wrestlers, Glen Joel and Doug Scalzi, a whole bunch of freshmen who had wrestled for me in junior high, and two girls, Debbie and Elaine.

The two young ladies were beautiful, shapely and well-endowed, and they were serious about wanting to wrestle. This was a time in the political history of the United States when the Equal Rights Amendment to the Constitution was being considered, and every little incident that had to do with women's rights had immediate national news coverage. No way was I going to say no to these girls. I knew if I did, the next week I'd have been depicted as a real bad guy on national television. Besides, I've always felt that anyone, man or woman, ought to have equal right to try anything. I felt men were genetically better prepared for wrestling, but let anyone try.

I did say the following when they asked to join the wrestling team: "Fine with me, but you have to go by the same rules as the rest of the team members."

"What do you mean by that?" they asked.

"Well, first, at matches you have to weigh in 'stripped down weight, shoulder-to-shoulder.' " I was quoting from the rule book of that year.

"What does that mean?" Elaine asked.

"Well, it means that at every match you girls would be standing around bare-naked with at least 22 bare-naked boys for weigh-ins." I figured that would give them a shock.

"Oh, okay, we can do that," Debbie said. Now I was shocked.

Regaining my composure, I quoted another rule. "You also would have to cut your hair so that it wouldn't be below your ears on the sides and couldn't touch a regular shirt collar in the back."

In unison and almost with a scream of distress, they both said, "We'd have to cut our hair?" Now they were shocked. Elaine and Debbie came to several practices, but never did cut their hair. Eventually they dropped out. The team was a little disappointed they quit. Everyone pretty well knew they wouldn't help the team that much; our 98-pound freshman could throw either one of them clear across the mat, but they were so nice-looking, practice was a much better place to be when they were there.

Both rules I quoted were at that time in the rule book. Since that time provisions have been added, both for weigh-ins and hair, that make it much easier for girls to wrestle and some do, but at that time those were the rules.

The girls never made it to the first match, but that first week the wrestling referees had a clinic and I heard that they tossed coins to see who would be the first referee to have a chance to weigh the two girls in. I never heard who won.

Chapter 42

Freshmen often are a trial to coach and yet at the same time funnier than a rubber crutch.

One of the freshmen this year was Andy Anders. He was a tough ranch kid. He never missed a practice, though he seemed to miss some things in his classes. He was always just on the edge of failing, but somehow was able to be passing just before eligibility check. (He later graduated from college as a civil engineer.)

One practice he came with his arm all bandaged up. It was wrapped with several layers of gauze and about three layers of athletic tape, but there he was at practice, doing the warm-up.

I called him to the side. "Andy, what's wrong with your arm?"

"Nothing, Coach, it's just a scratch."

"Why do you have all that tape on it?"

"It's really nothing, Coach, I'm fine."

"Let me look at it," I said.

"Coach, I'd have to take all the tape off and I don't want to miss any practice. Really, it's okay."

"Okay," I said reluctantly, "get back out there." Later I found out that he had been playing with his dad's .38 pistol and it discharged, traversing clear through the meaty part of his forearm. He didn't tell anyone but his brother, because he didn't want his dad to get mad at him. So he bandaged it himself and went to practice.

Andy had one peculiarity that was somewhat unusual for a hard-nosed cowboy. He never swore or used bad language. He had one expletive only. *Dirty word* was all he would say in stressful situations, but he could say *dirty word* with more passion than many of the best cussers. And we had a few of those on the team. I had a rule of no cussing during practice or at a match. I gave one warning, then I suspended a wrestler from the team. I had one heavyweight I had to suspend one time because he couldn't control himself. One wrestler I thought I would have to suspend was Adam McCabe, but somehow Adam could control himself on the mat. Off the mat and out of practice, he used every foul word in the English language in his common speech as if that was the only way he knew how to talk. I asked him about it, but he said, "That's the way my whole family talks."

Adam used to make fun of Andy's *dirty word*. "A real man knows what to say," Adam would taunt when Andy would passionately yell *dirty word*. Adam would get the whole team to make fun of Andy and his *dirty word*. But Andy was never swayed. *Dirty word* stayed his expletive of choice.

The tables were turned permanently though, one dual match. Adam, wrestling a tough match against Ninilchik, dislocated his elbow. Anyone who has seen a dislocated elbow knows that it is one of the ugliest injuries. The distortion of the joint is enough to make strong men upchuck from just seeing it, and the pain is distressing to say the least. Adam sat on the mat holding his arm as we gathered around. The pain was so bad that every muscle was shaking. This young man who knew every swear word in the book searched through his repertoire for one bad enough to use in this situation, and the expletive that came out was *dirty word*.

Chapter 43

"Coach, these tights won't stay up." It was Mark Hale, a freshman with a typical freshman question. A coach has to be patient with freshmen.

"They have tie strings to hold them up," I answered.

"Where?"

"Mark, you've got them on backwards. The tie string is in the back," I pointed out.

"Oh," Mark went back to his locker. We were dressing for our first match of the year against Kenai, our cross-borough rival. Mark was our varsity 112-pound wrestler. He had never wrestled a match before, but he was the only one on the team who could wrestle the 112-pound weight class. So here he was dressing for his first varsity match. I felt sorry for him; he was in one of those high school growth spurts that often happen to boys of that age. Such a time makes for a gangly, awkward stage in many boys' lives. Mark had those two characteristics doubly. Basically he couldn't chew gum and walk at the same time, let alone wrestle. However, I felt wrestling was good for him and he was our only 112-pounder so I was happy he was here. He also had a hard time catching onto new things, so his progress was slow in practice. To make matters worse for Mark, his opponent was Mike Kaiser, Kenai's returning state champion. And now, putting on the uniform was a challenge for Mark.

"Coach, they still won't stay up." Mark was back with another problem.

I surveyed his situation. "Mark, it's still on backwards, and now you've got it inside-out as well."

"You said backwards, so that's what I thought you meant."

"No, no, here, Mark, take them off." I turned the tights right-side-out and placed them correctly in front of him. "Mark, step into them this way. Here are the strings you tie to keep them up." A coach has to learn patience with freshmen.

The wrestling uniform of those days consisted of a pair of tights fastened with heel straps at the foot and tie strings at the waist, and a one-piece singlet, which is like a shirt and trunks attached. Wrestlers also wore a uniform-type warm-up suit outside of this while not wrestling.

I always had the team do some warm-up exercises on the mat together. It brought the team together and made them feel more like a team. I tried to have as many rituals associated with a match as I could, which helped the team understand they were a team, not 12 individuals. It has always been my firm belief that individuals will work harder, develop better, and climb higher when they know they are doing it for something greater than themselves.

Mark was out on the mat, his varsity warm-up suit on, and going through the warm-up ritual with the team. There were signs of worry on his passive white face. Mark always made the Homer fan section bigger. He was a somewhat plain young man, I thought, but this was not the thinking of the Homer girls. There were always 10 to 15 girls around him all the time. Maybe it was something about his dark wavy hair or his sky-blue eyes. Heavens, I'll never know, but he was the Pied Piper and Casanova of Homer all rolled into one. It certainly wasn't his body they were after. At least I don't think. It was hard to find a muscle anywhere on that Gandhi-like frame.

The wrestlers finished their warm-up and cleared the mat in the midst of cheers from the mostly female voices of the fans. Mark was the third match, so after the first match he took off his warm-up. I looked over and to my utter dismay, Mark had his singlet on backwards. It must have been horribly uncomfortable. It would be just a little worse than wearing a pair of Levi's backwards.

"Doug," I said to the team captain, "Can you take Mark to the locker room and get his singlet on right? He's got it on backwards."

"On backwards? How can you get it on backwards, Coach?"

"I don't know, but his is on backwards and you better hurry. It looks like Ormsby is pinning his kid," I urged.

Doug and Mark rushed out, and Ormsby did pin his opponent. Ormsby and his Kenai opponent shook hands. The referee raised the winner's hand and it was time for the next match.

Mike Kaiser, Kenai's returning state champ, stepped on the mat. He was almost five feet tall and his shoulders seemed as wide. The muscles rippled from his shoulder to his narrow waist, set on two tree trunks for legs. I knew he was short, but how all the muscle weighed no more than 112 pounds, I'll never know. Every bit of water in his body must have been sucked out by an Electrolux. He was ugly as well. If trolls ever existed, Mike Kaiser was a descendant.

Just about the time everyone was wondering where his opponent was, Mark came running out of the locker room, uniform on correctly. He tripped on the edge of the mat and almost recovered when he ran into the referee. Mark apologized, because he was a nice kid after all. The referee helped him to where he was supposed to be and blew the whistle to start the match.

Kaiser grabbed Mark's head with one hand, his foot with the other and bowled him over to his back. The referee, being in perfect position, counted, "One, two," and slapped the mat for the pin.

"That was a four-second pin, Steve," Coach Poindexter pointed out to me. I looked up and sure enough the score clock read, "1 minute, 56 seconds to go." It had taken Kaiser only four seconds to pin Mark.

"I think that is a world record," I said.

"It is a world record," Al informed me.

"Don't tell anyone and for sure don't tell Kenai." I wanted no one to know Homer was on the receiving end of a world's record like that. We all got up and patted Mark on the back and said things that we were supposed to say, like, "You'll get him next time," etc.

Mark never made the varsity team again; he always wrestled JV over the next few years, always with a large number of Homer girls there to cheer him on. He never lost his attraction to women, but those four seconds were his total varsity experience. I'm sure he eventually got over his awkwardness and could put on his uniform correctly, but I've lost track of where he is. I heard he was doing well in Florida. He was a good kid and I wish him the best. I just wonder how he could have become anything but a polygamist.

Chapter 44

Sometimes coaches forget the Mark Hales on their teams and only remember the greats. I expect that I don't remember everyone who wrestled for me during those years, but I do appreciate every one of them. The team was better when Mark was there, because he was there. And so with all of those who struggled, but not always made it to the top. They probably never realized it, but their contribution to the team was great.

One example was a boy by the name of Nathan Mouser. He was small by stature and build. He was well-muscled because of the hard work he did every summer fishing. He worked on his family's beach sites where most of the work was pulling nets and picking fish from them, all done by hand. He was not a fast or clever wrestler, but he was a hard worker. Nate was always doing and learning what he could in practice and if he ever missed practice, I don't remember it.

Because he was always there, he often wrestled varsity matches, winning a few. But in his junior and senior years some talented younger wrestlers joined the team and "Mouse," as he was affectionately called by the team, found himself a JV. He took it good-naturedly and was determined to work harder. As he did, the whole team was forced to work harder. He almost single-handedly raised the team to a higher level of conditioning. He deserved a reward, but I could think of no appropriate way to do it. Then came the Arctic Winter Games.

The Arctic Winter Games are a biennial set of athletic contests to which only arctic states and provinces are invited. It is usually the Canadian arctic provinces and Alaska that are included, but occasionally Norway, Sweden, Finland, Greenland and Iceland participate, and lately Siberia. The games include many winter sports such as skiing, biathlon and such, but also some Eskimo games such as "seal hop" and "one-legged high kick." There are also several indoor sports and wrestling is one of them.

I found myself given the responsibility of selecting the Alaska wrestling team. Coaches were not enthusiastic about sending their varsity team members to the Arctic Winter Games in the middle of the wrestling season.

For one thing, Alaska always won nearly every gold medal. Their kids would not get much tough competition. For another, it would weaken their varsity team during some crucial matches.

I hit on a plan to send JV wrestlers and was able to solicit some pretty fair JVs. I was also able to get Nathan Mouser a spot on the team. Nathan went to Dawson City, Yukon Territory, and wrestled with the Alaska team. He called me almost every night the entire week to tell me how Alaska was doing and he always finished with, "and, Coach, I won too." However, it wasn't until they posted the final winners in the Anchorage newspaper that I realized how well Alaska did. Alaska wrestlers had won 10 of the 13 gold ulus (an ulu is an Eskimo carving knife, given symbolically to the winners) and three silver ulus. One of the gold was given to Nathan Mouser. He was Arctic Winter Games champion for his weight class. That was Nathan's proudest moment, I know.

Nathan went to college at Texas Tech and wrestled with their club for a while. He earned an engineering degree, but came back to Homer to do what he had done his whole life. He is now a very successful local fisherman.

Chapter 45

One freshman that year was a story by himself. Jason Hill. He turned out to be one of the greatest wrestlers the state of Alaska ever had, but he never placed in regionals or state. As a freshman he wrestled a three-time state champ who was undefeated and unscored on. While in the bottom position, Jason stood up, stepped behind his opponent's near leg and executed a perfect standing Petersen to dump the strong Chugiak wrestler to his back. I was looking directly at the Chugiak boy and saw a look of total surprise and disbelief come over his usually impassive robot-like face. Of course, the Chugiak boy quickly recovered and crushed Jason, but that was an indication of how good Jason was to be in the future.

A week before regionals Jason was not at practice. "Where's Jason?" I asked the team.

"Oh, his dad took him fishing," someone said.

"Fishing?"

"Yah, his dad made him go herring fishing to Prince William Sound."

"Oh, okay. Couldn't he have waited a week?"

"No, Coach. Herring season is only a week, maybe two weeks long."

"Okay." It was easy to understand why he wanted to go. A deck-hand on a successful boat in Prince William Sound often made $40,000 to $50,000 in two weeks' work, but still Jason hadn't said anything to me and had let the team down.

The next year Jason came back at the start of practice. He was bigger, stronger and obviously going to be a help to the team.

"Jason, are you going to pull out at the end of the season again?" was the first question I asked him.

"No, Coach. I'm staying home and wrestling."

"I'm glad to hear it."

This year he was even better. He won 90 percent of his matches as a sophomore. He would have placed in regionals and probably in state, but the week before regionals:

"Where's Jason Hill?" I asked.

"His dad took him fishing," someone said.

Jason's junior year rolled around. He looked like Mohammed Ali, only white, this year.

"I want to wrestle again, Coach."

"Jason, you lied to me last year and what is to make me think it will be different this year? Don't you understand how much you let me and the team down when you left last year?"

"Yes, Coach," Jason hung his head like he was real sorry. "But this year my dad said he'd get a babysitter to take care of me and everything, so I won't have to go fishing."

Jason was living with his widower father. It was easy to understand why he may have had a problem the previous years. It still would have been much better for him to have communicated with me about the situation.

"You bring your dad in. When I have his word on it, then I'll let you wrestle."

Jason and Mr. Hill came in the next day.

"Jason wants to wrestle so I'm hirin' another hand and getting him a sitta' so he can stay and wrestle," Mr. Hill promised me in his heavy Maine accent.

"That's what I needed to know," I replied. "It's hard on the team and the coaches when a good wrestler like Jason is not there, especially for regionals and state."

"Well, he'll be the-uh this ye-ah," said Mr. Hill.

"Good to hear it." We shook hands and Mark came to practice.

Jason as a junior was awesome. He was absolutely fearless and unstoppable. One tournament in Seward he was wrestling in a finals match with an Adonis from Palmer named Stevensen. Stevensen was a blond Norse god, muscles from head to toe. Except for the blond hair he looked like Thor in the comic books. Stevensen shot in quickly and grabbed Jason's leg and lifted it high in the air so forcefully that Jason's head gear popped off. Then Stevensen did everything animally possible to tear Jason's leg off or throw him to the mat, whichever came first.

Jason, however, unworried about the predicament, still hopping on one leg (the match still in progress), reached down, picked up his head gear, snapped it on and then tossed Stevensen on his back and pinned him. I knew we had a state champion for sure.

The Monday before regionals early in the morning I received a call. There was a delay between interchanges, so I knew I was talking to someone on a marine radio. "Coach, this is Jason. My dad made me come fishing. We're on our way to Prince William Sound. I won't be able to wrestle at regionals or state."

"Can I talk to your dad?" I returned.

"Sure, he's right here."

"Mr. Hill, you promised you'd let Jason finish his wrestling season."

"Yep, I did, but things change. The sitta' got sick and the hi-ahd help didn't work out. So I'm takin' Jason."

"But doesn't your word mean anything?" I asked.

"A man's word means something when he signs on the dotted line, not until then. Jason wanted to come." Then he hung up.

Jason's senior year began. The first day of wrestling practice he showed up to my school room. I know it must have taken guts, but he was there.

"Coach, I want to wrestle."

"Jason, how can I trust you? Your father said you wanted to go fishing last year. Jason, you're a good wrestler. I want you on the team, but I can't let you let the team down like you did the last three years."

"Coach, what can I do? This year'll be different, I promise. I want to wrestle."

"Okay. This year we're going to have a contract signed by you, your dad and me, saying that you are going to finish the season."

"Oh, great, great," Jason said with relief. "I'll be glad to sign it and so will Dad."

And so the contract was signed. I even made the signature line dotted just for Mr. Hill.

What a great wrestler Jason was that year as well. Undefeated, a shoo-in for state champ, things looked good for Jason. Then came the Monday before regional tournament.

"Where's Jason?"

"His dad took him fishing."

I immediately went to the phone and got ahold of Jason's dad. "You signed a contract that you'd let him stay and finish the season."

"Jason wants to go, so I'm takin' him," was all the reply I got.

Revenge is sweet, though, even when you don't have anything to do with it. Jason and his dad spent the next three weeks on the beach in Cordova, because of a fisherman's strike. Jason missed regionals, state and the fishing season, and made very little, if any, money that season. In spite of these incidents, Jason and I stayed good friends. He would come up occasionally and wrestle with the team and when I was preparing for freestyle tournaments that I wrestled in, he would come up to the wrestling room and wrestle with me to help me get in shape. One tournament he decided to enter himself. He wrestled so well that he beat several college wrestlers. After that success he expressed that he would like to go to college and wrestle if he could get a scholarship. Again I tried to help him.

I called one of my old college teammates who was coaching a junior college and conned him into giving Jason a scholarship. We got all the paperwork ready at my home to sign. All he needed to do was come over and sign it. He never showed up. He took a job on a landing barge that was going to the Bering Sea.

Again, I had nothing to do with it, but revenge is sweet. Jason's skipper on the barge had seen Little Diomede Island lots of times, but had never seen Big Diomede Island. So he thought he'd just make a short detour and cruise on over to see if he could buy a t-shirt or something. Big Diomede is in Russian territorial waters and back then the Russians weren't nearly as friendly to the United States as they are now. At that time there was still a Berlin Wall.

The skipper, being a junior high drop-out, didn't recognize the red flag with the hammer and sickle on it, so he just kept cruising when the large warship steamed toward them at full speed. He got the message however, when they fired across his bow.

All the crew, including Jason, was taken into custody, hauled off to Russia and their boat confiscated. The crew was put in a Siberian prison where they spent the next six weeks. I understand the food wasn't real good, nor were they treated like honored guests. Eventually the Washington D.C. diplomats got them released. I still kid Jason about giving up his college scholarship so he could take a vacation in Russia.

Chapter 46

Two of the crazy freshmen that year were cousins, Dave Scalzi, Doug's younger brother, and Newby Ormsby. These two cousins were together all the time and when they got with their Hawaiian cohort, Eugene Ukulele, there was nothing they wouldn't do. Eugene was a bit older than they, but not their leader. He was more their collaborator.

Dave was a strong, tough little guy who wrestled 98- or 105-pound weight classes. One practice he wrenched his neck so he couldn't move it without pain. The doctor said it was just muscle strain and would be better in a week or so. So Dave kept wrestling. He went through an entire week of practice and school with his head tilted at a 45-degree angle to the left. He wrestled his matches that week the same way, and he won.

Newby was built almost opposite of Dave. Where Dave was blond with short hair, Newby had thick curly black hair. Where Dave was short and well-muscled, Newby was taller and wiry. Newby's hair looked like Harpo Marx's, only black, and he naturally walked like Charlie Chaplin. He always smiled, which was disconcerting to his opponents. Perhaps the most entertaining part of any Homer match was to see Newby walk, Charlie Chaplin-style, out on the mat, grinning from ear to ear, shake hands with his opponent, pin him and then walk back off the mat in the side-to-side rocking motion of the silent-movie star.

One of the pre-match rituals I had with the team was what I called "dark room." I would bring the team into a room where we could talk. I'd give them a pep talk, then turn all the lights off and help them to mentally see themselves wrestling the match they wanted to wrestle. I felt it was a good way to overcome many mental roadblocks young men of this age often have that keep them from success. I also took time to let those who were praying men have a quiet time for a personal, private prayer if they so chose.

We usually chose the laundry room as our dark room. It was next to the locker room and convenient, but there was not always a lot of room for the whole team. So Newby, being fairly small and flexible, would climb in the large dryer for our "dark room" time. There seemed to be nothing dangerous about it, so I let him do it.

One time, during one of my stirring pep talks, Dave reached up before Newby knew what was going on, shut the dryer's glass door and turned on the dryer. Before I knew what was happening, I looked up and there was Newby's face glued to the glass door, going around and around in the dryer like a frog in a blender. He went around four or five times before I got over and let him out.

"Hey, that was fun. Can I do it again?"

I knew where that would go if I let him go again. I'd have everyone from Dave, our 98-pounder, to Glen Joel, our heavyweight, trying to climb in the dryer for a ride. I never let Newby in the dryer again, but I'll always remember his surprised face going around and around as it peered out the dryer door.

Newby loved his little digs at his opponents, all good-natured in a mean sort of way. One dual match at Seward we arrived about an hour before weigh-ins. All the team was on weight, so we just had to wait with mostly nothing to do. The Seward wrestler in Newby's weight wasn't so lucky. He was dressed in two sweat suits and a heavy parka, running around and around the gym. He was obviously overweight and trying to sweat off a few pounds.

You can tell when a wrestler is close to the breaking point in losing weight. There are white circles of fear around his eyes and ears, and his skin looks kind of shriveled up like a dried prune. This Seward boy was at that point, but he kept running. We all sympathized with him; most of us had been there. In that situation all you can think about is water, cool clear water, or orange juice or milk, anything to drink. You fantasize about a fairy godmother coming to your relief with a big pitcher of Kool-Aid. So we sympathetically watched while he ran.

Finally weigh-in time came. Newby weighed in first, immediately followed by the Seward runner. Newby easily made weight and immediately popped open a can of Gatorade. It is not unusual for wrestlers to do that after weigh-in; in fact, after weigh-in, the locker room usually turns into a lunchroom.

The Seward boy, however, stepped on the scale. "One-quarter pound over. You have one half-hour to make weight," was the referees' announcement. Utterly dejected, he stepped off the scale, knowing that one-quarter pound was not much to lose in a half-hour, but so disappointed he had not made it yet.

Newby said, "Here, buddy, have a Gatorade," and very sympathetically offered him the rest of his drink. A big smile of thankfulness lit up the Seward boy's face for an instant. Then he realized what a friendly enemy Newby was being as he gently pushed away Newby's hand, the dejected look even more pronounced on his face as he realized how much weight just one little drink would put back on him. The sad footnote was that although the Seward boy made weight, Newby pinned him in about 30 seconds.

Chapter 47

Making weight resulted in some of the most bizarre aspects of wrestling. There were at that time 12 weight classes to accommodate all sizes of wrestlers. What is supposed to happen is that each wrestler is to always weigh his natural weight and wrestle in that weight class. Two facts destroy this ideal situation. First: even doctors don't realize how much a teenager may vary in weight during the day. Weight may fluctuate five to seven pounds in any given day, sometimes even more. Second: it is easy to change weight by 10 to 15 pounds by limiting water intake for extended periods and by inducing sweating. Wrestlers learn quickly that they can lose a few pounds of water and drop to a lower weight class with little effect on their performance. To wrestle in a lower weight class is a big advantage. The less body weight to move around — yourself and your opponent's — translates into a large amount of energy saved and strength needed.

Losing a few pounds of body weight is usually a healthy thing for American kids who usually have 15 to 20 percent body fat. Fat helps performance in wrestling very little. The most efficient wrestler is one with a minimum of body fat. That is why most wrestlers, when they are in fighting condition, could do well in body-building contests.

Most of the time young men are fairly sensible about losing weight, with some guidance from a well-informed coach. However, mothers are often the hardest obstacle to overcome.

"What do you mean you're only having seven pancakes this morning? You always eat eight pancakes. Are you trying to lose weight for wrestling again? You'll starve to death and die if you keep this up."

"Mom, really, that's all I want."

"Eat another pancake. One more won't hurt you and I don't want my sweetheart starving to death."

It takes a strong personality to lose weight when you have a mother like that, especially if you're a little hungry.

There are three common ways to make weight: diet, lose water and cheat. There are thousands of ways to diet. Nearly all of them work, but very few are good for wrestlers who want to keep muscle and lose fat. For those young men who do have excess fat, I always recommend that they eat the meals their mothers fix, but eat only one-half what they usually do and never take seconds. I also urge them to take vitamins and avoid eating fatty food. However, some wrestlers occasionally go on fad diets and try quick reductions just as I did when I wrestled.

One time after a two-year layoff from college I found myself 20 pounds overweight and trying to wrestle again. I had almost no money for food, but my dad had donated to my college fund half a buck deer he'd shot and wrapped up. So I ate venison. Someone told me that meat and grapefruit juice was a good combination. For the next two months I consumed nothing but grapefruit juice and venison. I lost 18 pounds in a month and a half. That was drastic. I had one wrestler who lost weight by eating only air-popped popcorn for supper, another who lived completely on dried oatmeal, no milk, no sugar. Both of these boys were state place winners.

The second method is losing water. High school rules prohibit using steam rooms, hot tubs, hot showers, diuretics or any artificial methods of losing water weight. But sweating, that is perfectly legal if you exercise to do it. So often a wrestler, if he finds himself overweight for the weight class he wants to wrestle in, dons two sets of sweats, a big coat and runs, wrestles or does calisthenics until he has sweat enough to make weight. It takes a pint of sweat to lose one pound of body weight. What is amazing is that it is not uncommon for a wrestler to lose five pounds within a couple hours. Of course, as soon as he drinks that liquid he again weighs his original weight.

The third method of making weight is cheating. This happens even in wrestling. Wrestlers are as creative about cheating to make weight as most good shysters are about getting people to give them their money.

One method wrestlers occasionally use is to put a hand on top of the scale's upright as if to steady themselves as they step on the scale, then just leave the hand resting on the upright, which sometimes is the difference of three pounds. Another common method is to have a teammate stand very close to the scale when they are being weighed in and having him stick his thumb under one cheek of his teammate's buttocks without the referee seeing and then lifting up. One is much lighter when he is being lifted by the buttocks. Another method is to stand close to the front of the scale and stick your big toe out far enough that it touches the scale's upright and then push down. This method is good for two pounds or so. It takes a sharp and experienced referee to catch all the possible ways to cheat. That's why at nearly every weigh-in both coaches are there just to occasionally point out something the referee missed.

I had seen the big-toe method of cheating several times, but a Kenai boy almost fooled the referee and me with it one time.

Kenai was down for a dual match. As happens to almost every team once during the winter, the Kenai team was devastated by the flu. Several of their key wrestlers couldn't make the trip. They had a stand-in 177-pound wrestler who had to make weight for them to have a chance to beat us. However, he was two pounds overweight. Everyone else weighed in and this boy came back to re-weigh; only this time he sat down cross-legged on the scale. He was right on weight.

Bruce, the referee, said, "Just a minute, stand up." The Kenai boy stood up and was promptly two pounds over. "You're still two pounds over," said Bruce.

"But I can make it sitting down." He sat down and sure enough he was on weight.

This is scientifically impossible. You weigh the same standing up or sitting down. My mouth dropped open. So did Bruce's. Bruce turned to me. "What do you think, Coach?"

It was at that moment I saw the big toe sticking out from under the crossed legs, touching the scale upright.

"Sure, let him wrestle," I said, "if he can make weight without his toe touching the scale like that." He couldn't, and so he didn't wrestle and we won the match.

There are a few bizarre ways of losing weight that really don't fit in any category. Losing blood really helps you lose weight. I became aware of this in college. Being a starving college student, I found a clinic that would buy blood. They would pay me $20 once a month for a pint of my blood. At that time $20 was almost enough food money for a month. So every month like clockwork I was there selling my blood. They always gave me a cup of orange juice and said, "No strenuous exercise for 24 hours." I usually drank the orange juice, collected the $20 and then went to wrestling practice where the exercise was always strenuous. It never seemed to affect me at practice except I was always one pound lighter than usual after practice. And it was a pound that didn't come back the next day. As I look back, I realize how foolish I was, but when you're that age you think you're indestructible.

I was never as foolish as the wrestler I saw at the NCAA championships my senior year. I'd weighed in and was getting dressed when I noticed this black kid from some school in California. I'm not sure why I noticed him, maybe because he looked like a tank, and yet he was in my weight class. He stepped on the scale. I was secretly glad the referee said, "You're over about a quarter pound." The tank seemed undisturbed. A quarter pound is not a lot to lose, but instead of putting his sweats on, he walked over to his clothes, picked up a towel and sat down. He then very forcefully punched himself in the nose.

"This guy is crazy," I said to myself. "I hope I don't have to wrestle him. A crazy tank might be formidable."

I continued to watch, it took a couple good clouts to the nose, but finally he began bleeding from both nostrils. He sat on the bench and watched the blood fall onto his towel. I was so taken by what was happening that I stopped everything I was doing, but tried not to stare, at least with my mouth open. Soon (about seven or eight minutes later) he wiped his nose, stepped back on the scales and made weight.

Hair weighs almost nothing, but I've seen it help a person make weight several times. Even part of an ounce sometimes is enough to tip the scale so that a wrestler makes weight.

Mark Degraffenried had an unusual way of making weight. His method was as scientific as tarot cards, but for him it worked. If he was overweight by less than a quarter of a pound, he'd stand on his head for one minute, immediately jump up on the scale and he'd make weight. No one yet has explained why this method worked for him. For others who tried it, it didn't work nearly as well, but for Mark it worked every time. I never got used to that naked body standing upside-down in the locker room, but if it worked for Mark, what the heck, let him do it.

Mark was a fair wrestler, never great, but he was a great sculptor. Several of the works he created during his high school years were sold at a good price. He now is making a fair living at turning out some of the best sculpture I've ever seen. I'm not much of an art critic, but when Mark was a high school student he sculpted a scene of a hunter who had just discovered he'd shot the last unicorn. The detail and pathos on the hunter's face and obvious agony his whole body depicted was truly moving to me. I'm not easily moved by art, but that was one of the few art pieces that has moved me. Today you can see one of Mark's bronze statues at the Seafarer's Memorial on the Homer Spit. I believe anyone who has been around the sea can see Mark has captured in statue form the spirit of the seafarer.

Chapter 48

This year we had several kids who gave us coaches fits with weight. One was Allen Toungelite. One Thursday evening after practice he weighed in one pound underweight, even though he had struggled all week with his weight. He was ecstatic.

"Coach, what can I eat?"

"Eat a small meal — not more than two pounds. And drink no more than a pint. And you will be just right for weigh-in tomorrow. You are one pound under now, your body will naturally lose about two pounds overnight as you sleep, so you will be just right on weight," I counseled him.

"Coach, I'm afraid to eat anything. So I think I will only drink a little water." It is typical of a high school student to ask for your advice and then tell you what he is going to do anyway.

I tried again. "Eat a little supper, but don't overeat, and you'll be right on," I said, and left it at that.

The next day Allen weighed in three pounds overweight.

"What did you eat?" I asked in exasperation.

"I only had a carrot, honest, Coach."

The whole team was standing around. Heath was the first to speak up. "A three-pound carrot?" He held up his hands three feet across, and of course the whole team laughed.

A few days later Bob Stonum came up to me with his hands behind his back. Bob was a rotund sort of wrestler with a round pleasant face and great sense of humor. His one claim to fame this year in wrestling was that he had lost so much weight he could now tie his shoes by himself.

"Coach," he said, all serious, "Coach, I've gained five pounds and all I ate was an apple." He pulled out from behind his back an enormous apple. It was the size of a pumpkin. Its stem was as big as a pencil. How it ever grew on a tree I'll never know, but after seeing it I gave Allen's three-pound carrot story a little more credibility.

Allen Toungelite was a junior. He was a fine wrestler who had really come of age this year. He was named outstanding wrestler at the Homer Winter Carnival Tournament and was one of the best in the state at his weight class. These were the years of the first "Rocky" movies; Allen with his square jaw, wavy black hair and deep-set eyes looked a little like Sylvester Stallone in a skinny sort of way. I never noticed it too much until the regional tournament. Allen, with his typical weight problem, put on a hooded sweatshirt and began running around Wasilla's indoor track. Someone from the Kenai team looked up and yelled:

"Hey, guys, it's Rocky!"

"Yah, it is Rocky!" said another.

The whole bunch of the crazy Kenai guys jumped up and started running behind Allen chanting, "Go, Rocky, go! Go, Rocky go!" and yelling, "We're behind you Rocky, go!" Allen turned redder and redder, and not from his exertion.

The footnote to that incident was that the next year when we went to our first tournament in Seward a nice-looking young girl came up to me and asked where "Rocky" was.

I had forgotten about the incident at the previous year's regional tournament, so I replied, "Rocky? Rocky who?"

"Rocky Toungelite," she said.

"Oh, you mean Allen Toungelite. He's in another van." I then yelled, "Rocky, oh, Rocky, there is someone here to see you."

"Rocky? Who is Rocky?" Peter Beneboe asked.

But Glen caught on right away and turned to Allen, elevating his voice an octave, and said, "Oh, Rocky, where's my Rocky?" This was followed by a bunch of guffaws and derogatory remarks from the rest of the team about the name "Rocky."

In the next town the following week, we went to the school only to be met by another nice-looking young lady asking,"Where's Rocky?" And so it was the rest of the season. Allen always was a ladies man, but now that he had the name "Rocky," he had a girl in every port.

Chapter 49

This year's wrestling season was fun and yet, in the end, disappointing. We had so many freshmen on the team we started out poorly, but as they learned and worked, they could accomplish anything. We were a school of about 280 students, competing against the best and biggest in the state.

We didn't always win, but we always made our presence known. At the Homer Winter Carnival against eight tough teams we placed second, losing only to Palmer. We later soundly trounced Palmer 56-12 at their hometown match. We wrestled Service, an Anchorage school of 3,000 students. Year after year they had more than 100 students turn out for wrestling. This year no team had won more than three weights against them. We lost the match, but we won four weights against them. It looked like we were going to be the small-school state championship team.

This year for first time they were going to give a small-school state championship trophy for the approximately 200 schools in Alaska which had under 400 students, and a large-school state championship for the schools above 400 students. However, everyone wrestled everyone at state and the small school which had the highest score was small-school champ and whoever had the best score overall became the large-school champ. Very few of us had the illusion that a small school might score the most. In the history of Alaska wrestling, no small school had even scored in the top 10, let alone challenged for the top two spots.

Wrestling is probably the hardest of any of the sports for a small school to do well at against a large school. It happens in basketball that a small school occasionally beats the very best, but in basketball a school needs to come up with five top athletes to field an outstanding team. Football is much harder because you must find 11 topnotch players in the smaller number of students to pick from. But in wrestling at that time, you needed 12 outstanding athletes, but also they all had to be in different weight classes. If you had two great athletes in the same weight class you could only use one. In basketball, football, track, etc., two good athletes weighing the same are still two good athletes you can use.

An oddity about this system of declaring small-school state champions occurred in our region. For some reason the powers-that-be decided the four small schools in our region had to wrestle against the eight large schools in our region at a regional tournament to qualify for the state tournament. All other approximately 200 small schools qualified by wrestling only against small schools.

What this meant was although that year we could easily beat in any dual match any of the 200-plus small schools, it would be tough for us to get enough wrestlers to state to be able to score many points at the state tournament.

However, we stepped into the regional tournament with the enthusiasm and optimism that only a bunch of freshmen can. Regionals turned out to be the toughest dogfight of the year. The kids wrestled great, but when all the shouting and wrestling finished, when the dust cleared and everyone counted the money at the table, Homer only qualified two for state. Doug Scalzi as a junior took second, losing a close match in the finals to the Kenai returning state champ. He was obviously going to go far at state. Glen Joel wrestled to a third-place position against the strongest heavyweight class in the year. Allen Toungelite was injured early in the tournament with a separated sternum and did not place. Five other wrestlers placed fourth. So we took third in the tournament of 12 teams which was great for a small school but, with only two going to state, was not good for our state championship chances. Indeed it turned out even worse.

Glen lost his first two matches at state and Doug picked up a bad flu bug about mid-week. He tried to wrestle, but couldn't finish his first match. He spent the rest of the tournament in bed with a fever.

It was a disappointing end, but not a disappointing season. We wrestled well for a young team and the kids knew it. They also accomplished my number one goal for any team. They had fun wrestling.

Hillary, our manager, planned an end-of-the-year wrestling party. She planned food for 30 people, and indeed 30 of us showed up. When I saw the spread, I asked Hillary how she came up with the amounts. There were sandwiches from one end of the table to the other — sandwiches with lunch meat, with peanut butter, with tuna fish, with egg salad. There were vegetables and fruit galore, large pots of chili and clam chowder. There were bags and bag of chips, rows and rows of pop cans, and ice cream everywhere.

Hillary cheerfully answered, "I just figured what I could eat and then multiplied by 30." She must have been able to eat a lot, because 30 teenage wrestlers who no longer had to worry about weighing in got through only about a third of the food before all were lying on the floor groaning, with bellies bulging and belts unbuckled.

Perhaps the most rewarding event of the season happened the next Monday. I was walking by the office when Mr. Linn crooked his finger at me.

"Oh, no," I said to myself. "What is he going to chew on me about now?"

"Steve," he started. Being called by my first name was something new. "Steve, I said I'd be watching you very carefully during this wrestling season and I did. What I had heard about you as a wrestling coach before was wrong. You've done a fine job with the wrestlers this year. Keep it up."

I was shocked. I did manage to say, "Thank you" before I left. I've always respected Mr. Linn because he was able to overcome his previous prejudice. From that point on, anything that I asked for, Mr. Linn did whatever he could to expedite it.

Chapter 50

About this time the Club Bar burned down. The Yah Sure Club had burned down two weeks earlier and some thought "Christian fanatics" were plotting to destroy all the "dens of inequity" in Homer. No evidence of a conspiracy ever came to light, but nevertheless the tragedy was real and painful to many people in town.

There were just about as many churches in town as bars. I understand this happened early in the town's history. There were getting to be so many bars that the city council passed an ordinance that there could be no more bars than churches. Suddenly several churches were built, all with money from collection plates passed around in local bars.

Still, the loss of two of the biggest and most successful bars in Homer was of great concern to many of the beer drinkers in Homer, a category not of small numbers. They all rejoiced when the Club Bar owner struck back by building a bigger and better bar on the ashes of the old one.

The old Club Bar was not much more than a large one-room log house. Rebuilt, it became a large bar with dance floor, café and lounging area upstairs. There was little protest against it except a few letters to the editor about the evils of alcohol and bars in general. But then they painted "The Scene" on the front of the newly completed bar and Homer came unglued.

"The Scene" was commissioned by the Club Bar owner to be a representation of a Phoenix rising from the ashes, more beautiful than ever, as a symbol of the way the Club Bar was also rising out of its ashes. Homer has always been a town not only of right-wing Christians, but also of the artsy-craft people who love art for art's sake.

So a proper artist who was a local client of the Club Bar painted "The Scene." He did a pretty good job, I guess (being, like I am, a person who has never known what real art is). However, in "The Scene" he showed Adam and Eve watching the rising of the Phoenix. It was Adam and Eve still in the garden, with graphic depictions of their genitalia.

Boy, were people upset. Certain Christian churches had people stake out the Club Bar with signs protesting the "obscene" painting. Local patrons ignored them or accused them of wanting a closer look. Sometimes the shouting and fist-waving got intense. Soon people from the local arts council were also marching up and down in front of the bar with placards in support of an artist painting anything he wanted.

154

The *Homer News* (a newspaper run by those on the local arts council) published several editorials in support of the painting. Soon the *Homer News* was not big enough for the letters to the editor, both for and against "The Scene." The local radio station, KBBI, a public radio station (also run by the arts council people) ran debates, editorial comments and man-on-the-street interviews on the same subject. A Christian radio station started up just to combat the "misinformation."

Homer always was a town with diverse opinions, but "The Scene" had brought everyone out of the woodwork. Every mailbox in the city and surrounding area received a flyer which pointed out that "The Scene" was the first of many indications of evil in the land and all the evil was started by "the Jews." I read the pamphlet, but never understood the connection between evil and "the Jews."

Pretty soon people became almost violent. Someone threw a bottle of paint at "The Scene." It missed any naked being, but caught the poor Phoenix square on the beak, making it appear that he was vomiting in the midst of his resurrection. There was one anonymous letter to the editor that said he'd "burn down the Club Bar again" unless they got rid of that painting, and then he'd go after the *Homer News*. Things were getting ugly.

All the community excitement over "The Scene" terminated in a community-wide meeting held in the local elementary school gym which was the only place big enough. There must have been 900 people there, almost a third of every man, woman and child in Homer and the surrounding area. Never in the history of Homer had that many people been in one place before this night, and every one of them had to speak. Speakers were loudly applauded by some, and booed and catcalled by others. One guy showed up in shorts, a mask and a red cape. I never did understand why he was parading around, but he made the meeting a little more scary.

After about three or four hours of testimony, the Club Bar owner, Madge, got up and said that while we were talking, the artist was painting some bushes to make Adam and Eve look more presentable for public viewing. Then everyone was happy except the arts council. They wanted to talk more. Indeed, KBBI and the *Homer News* had several more editorials about how this great art had to be modified because of the "straightjacket minds" of some people. Everyone pretty well ignored the editorials.

It wasn't long until the Club Bar went belly-up and was sold. It is now Alice's Champagne Palace and the new owner painted over "The Scene." Seems he didn't think the art was that good, but I hear from some that Alice's is still a den of iniquity.

Chapter 51

At our new house we had managed to establish a nice lawn and garden. Contrary to what I had first felt about Alaska being all ice and snow, Homer is a rather comfortable place to live. Gardens grow quite well if you limit yourself to planting root crops and things like lettuce and cabbage. Potatoes grown in Homer, I soon discovered, are the best in the world. I grew up in Idaho and loved Idaho potatoes, but Alaska potatoes are a cut above them. They pick up something naturally from the soil that makes them more flavorful and sweeter somehow. Alaska potatoes are great.

Berries are also prolific in this area. We planted a patch of raspberries and they soon spread to a rather large area in back of our garden. The natural flora of the area also grew. Everything grows so tall in Alaska that it was very difficult for us to find and/or cultivate the raspberries. I hit on a plan I'd heard about somewhere and fenced them in, and then in the summer we would raise 20 or so chickens in the fence. The chickens scratched around the roots of the raspberries and ate all the weeds, but never touched a raspberry leaf. Sometimes they would jump up and eat some of the lower raspberries, but nothing more. The chickens kept all the other weeds pretty well eaten down, but the raspberries flourished and were much easier to pick.

Nina always made very fine raspberry jelly from the patch, but this summer her jelly turned out fabulous. I had never tasted a more exquisite jelly in my life. There was the perfect amount of flavor, tartness and sweetness. The clarity and color were beautiful. The texture could not be more perfect for spreading on bread either. If a jelly ever reached perfection, in my opinion, this summer's raspberry jelly was it.

I just had to enter it in the local fair. About 45 miles north of Homer was Ninilchik where they held the Kenai Peninsula Fair. That is where we would enter a winning jelly. All the judges had to do was taste it and I knew they'd be as enthralled as I was with Nina's jelly.

Nina didn't want me to, but I was insistent on entering it in the fair. I'd been to the Idaho county fairs and had been in 4-H and knew just what to do. So I took her beautiful jelly up to the fair. When I got there I signed up and was directed to display it in the canning section.

"Are there subdivisions of the canning section?" I asked.

The lady in charge of signing me up was one of those cheerful people, with gray hair and round glasses braced on her nose, who always seems ready to help at functions like this.

"No," she laughed. "We've always had the jelly in the canning section. Oh, my, what a lovely color to that jelly. Is it raspberry?"

I assured her it was.

"Oh, my, my, I'm sure it will do well," she said.

Of course I knew she was right. Buoyed by her vote of confidence, I made my way to the display area. Now I only needed to wait three days and Nina would have the blue ribbon she deserved. Maybe even the overall purple grand prize.

Three days later the whole family made its way to the fair. We couldn't wait for our wonderful mother and wife to receive her first great cooking award. I had convinced all those young impressionable children that their mother's jelly was the best in the world, not just in the fair. Nina, however, was skeptical that she would receive anything at all.

We walked into the canning section. And there, prominently displayed, were the winners. My heart sank a little when I saw the purple ribbon did not belong to Nina's jelly. We checked blue and red and white ribbons, but none were Nina's jelly. In fact, all four had been won by "home-brews."

Prominently displayed with each of the ribbons was the empty bottle of each of the homemade beers. Surely they must have divided the canning section into categories. I checked back at Nina's jelly display. Nothing, no ribbon, no judge's comments. No one had bothered to even taste it. I looked around and no one's jelly, or fish, or vegetables, or any canning product had been tasted except the home-brews. And every home-brew bottle was empty. I don't know who the judge was, but he could sure drink a lot of beer. He must've enjoyed the home-brew so much he was either too full — or couldn't find the other canning products.

The family had a fun time at the fair anyway, even if Nina didn't get a blue ribbon.

Chapter 52

Our family was growing. Rainbow was over a year old this summer. She had managed to say her first phrase, "No way, Jose!" and she knew the proper time to use it. Also, our fifth child, Tamara, was born. She was another beautiful little girl.

Our home was a nice place to be. We landscaped it and made a large lawn on the half-acre, had a nice garden and chickens. It was a regular ranch. There was one problem however. Three times we had to have the septic system dug up and redone. The clay soil of Homer did not allow for the seepage of wastewater into the ground. It just seemed to come right to the top and then go wherever it could. After the third dig we compromised with the septic system and just let it run off the corner of our property. Everyone else had the same problem in our neighborhood, so we were all tolerant. We had to inform the kids to stay away from the "sewer," but we had no trouble with them doing just that inasmuch as it smelled and looked so nasty.

However, in the middle of the winter when I informed the family I was going to Seward for a wrestling tournament, all three of the older children came to me as a unit, very concerned.

"Dad, why would you go to the 'sewer' for a wrestling tournament?" It took me a while to explain the difference between sewer and Seward. It is nice that the city of Homer now has a sewer system and our "sewer" problem is eliminated.

Chapter 53

It has been my habit since college to awake between 5 and 6 a.m. and run two to three miles just to keep myself in general fitness. Sometimes I'm adventurous and run five miles. These are generally dull times with very few incidents. There are few cars on the roads at this time of day and most dogs haven't awakened yet. The dogs that are awake at that time seem to enjoy the exercise also and follow me down the road, tongues (like mine) happily hanging out, and enjoying the morning air. Several times dogs have followed me all the way home and we had to look on their tags and call the owners to come and haul them back home.

I think because of the lack of dogs in our yard on a regular basis, a couple of cow moose have made our lawn their home for most of the winter. They also probably enjoy the lush grass which is available off and on most of the winter. We have taken numerous pictures of these moose just outside our window grazing on our lawn. Sometimes they have their newborn calves. One time Nina opened the back door and was nearly scared to death by a moose that had climbed up on the back porch exploring for some tidbit to eat. Generally you only see moose very early in the morning. They seem to hide in the woods during the daylight hours.

One morning as I was running, I startled a couple of moose who ran out on the road and then kept pace just ahead of me down the road for about a half-mile. They didn't seem to be belligerent. They finally got tired of the jog and turned off the road as I continued.

After one morning's five-mile run I was feeling particularly giddy, which happens when one has been so foolish as to put in that much effort at so early an hour. Adrenaline was affecting my brain as might some of the illicit drugs that are illicit because they make you particularly stupid during use. As I finished my run, I saw that there in the front yard was the cow moose. My first drug-induced thought was "I think I'll just go pet that moose."

I had been raised around a lot of rangy, skittish horses and I'd learned how to get close to them when they were not sure they wanted you around. It's just a matter of having patience and approaching so slowly that they never realize how close you are. When they start to back off, stop until they have settled down, and then again begin slowly approaching them. I used the same method with this wild cow moose. I'm sure she didn't know what this crazy human was doing or why, but with time and patience I got so close to her that I slowly reached out and just brushed the hair on her nose.

Her front foot came up so swiftly, I had no chance to dodge. I saw that razor-sharp hoof miss my face, chest and belly by a fraction of an inch. She had warned me well. I was suddenly a sober man. My thought was, "This was a real stupid idea." I slowly retreated to the house and my senses.

Once we had a dog for a short period of time, but he didn't work out. We've always had cats, and they don't chase moose away, so we still have moose on our lawn. When Rebekah was about five, we were talking about food and I was making the point that people eat people food and cats eat cat food. "You'd never eat cat food, would you?" I asked.

"No way," was Becky's reply. "I only like dog food." Then she admitted that a few years earlier she and some friends used to get in the garage and eat the dog's food. I had always wondered what happened to the leftover dog food when we gave our dog away.

Chapter 54

I am one of those comical people who have gout. Of course, gout is only comical to those who don't have it. Gout is a disorder of the blood. Some people have a poor system of eliminating uric acid from the blood. When uric acid is not properly eliminated from the blood, it builds up, crystallizes and is pumped into a lower joint, usually the great toe, causing excruciating pain.

The first time I found that I had the malady was as a college student. I thought I'd broken my toe in wrestling practice. I hobbled into the student medical center with the help of my wife and a pair of crutches. It hurt to move the foot, it hurt to not move the foot, it hurt to smile. I was moaning in pain and every once in a while I'd scream in agony. I think Nina was a little ashamed I was being such a baby over a little toe pain, but, oh, it hurt. I was directed to sit down. I did, after a scream of pain as I touched my toe to the floor while I was trying to shuffle over to a chair. I finally was able to sit where I continued my moaning.

The nurse came to me, clipboard in hand, and began: "Your name?"

"Steven Wolfe," I said, followed by a short moan.

"Address?" she continued.

"154 West, 400 North," followed by a long moan.

"Telephone number?"

"235-4040," followed by a longer moan.

"Social Security number?"

I couldn't take it any longer. After a scream, I yelled, "A guy comes in here dying and you ask him his Social Security number?" And I moaned again. The nurse got excited and started running around to get some help. Nina, not about to admit she had come in with me, went into another room. Somehow the doctor got me settled down and medicated enough to calm the worst of the gout pain. Then he told me what I had and how to care for it.

"Now, these yellow pills you have to take every day for the rest of your life. This is like diabetes. Once you have it, you've got it for the rest of your life." He continued his lecture. "Gout is painful. In itself it's not so bad, but it can lead to liver problems and kidney failure if not treated, not to mention amputation of the big toes like they used to do in the olden days."

"For the rest of my life?" I wailed. I was not one for taking pills. I felt like pills were for old people. I was 25 at the time.

"Don't take your pills and the 'rest of your life' might be short and painful," the doctor replied.

So I took the pills when I remembered. Sometimes I didn't remember, which was painful. But a bigger problem was that my body was great at compensating for additional chemicals present. Soon I was back in the doctor's office. The yellow pills weren't working.

"Boy, it's a good thing you don't use alcohol," the doctor said. "With your ability to adjust to chemicals, you'd make a great alcoholic." And he gave me some white pills.

And so the experimenting began. A medication would work for a while, and then it wouldn't. I had medication that made me sick, but didn't help. I had pills that put blisters the size of silver dollars on the inside of my mouth so it was too painful to eat or drink anything. I had doctors try to control my gout with diet, and fail. I also got a lot of advice from non-doctors. It seems that gout has as many cures as cancer, and all of them are just as effective as are the cures for cancer. But I think the most interesting pills the doctor gave me was colchicine. Colchicine is a deadly poison and was used by Byzantine spies quite extensively in the seventh and eighth centuries A.D. One time this poison was administered to a rival king who didn't die, but his gout was cured. Thereafter its medicinal use for curing gout made it just as useful as it was for killing people.

The directions for taking this medication were: "Take one every half-hour until nausea, vomiting, diarrhea occur, or pain ceases." I'd take the pills on the half-hour until I was vomiting, had diarrhea and was so nauseated I didn't care that I had gout. Then the pain went away. It was wonderful. I only used the cure a couple times though.

This school year was a gout year. The doctors were still trying to find something successful to work for me. In the meantime I had gout in my knee, my ankle, my toe, my other knee. Thankfully only one joint at a time. I felt like the medicine was chasing the gout around, but never quite catching it.

The doctors continued the experiments through December and finally somehow the gout was hog-tied and no longer a problem for the rest of the year. Although it has occasionally returned through the years, now gout is not particularly a problem for me. Fortunately, after years of experimentation (all of it painful) my family doctor has found some medications that seems to work and that my body has not built up a tolerance to. It is so nice to be free of the pain, and now I'm old so taking pills every day doesn't bother me nearly so much.

Chapter 55

I wasn't a whole lot of help in football this year because of my gout attacks, but the team did well. We had an equipment donation from a fisherman who had a good fishing year, and the kids had a lot of fun. We even had a faculty-versus-kids game which everyone enjoyed. Needless to say, football was well-received by the school at this time although just a club.

The most notable event of the football year was Homer's first "homecoming." It was a Hillary project. Hillary was my wrestling manager from the year before. This year she had worked her way into the volunteer manager position of the football team and was a very good manager. Of course, we now had cheerleaders and she helped them out as well.

The cheerleader sponsor thought we ought to have a homecoming dance so she put one together. Hillary volunteered to get the food since that was her specialty. The cheerleaders were going to take care of other things, but as time went along, Hillary volunteered for more and more. When the cheerleaders went down to the Elks Hall after school to decorate for the dance, it was all done. Hillary had skipped school and spent all day decorating. She'd lined up and lined out a band. She had the food ready. She'd done everything.

"This is wonderful, Hillary, but we were coming to decorate," Suzie said.

"It's okay," said Hillary. "I had the time, so I went ahead."

Hillary continued, "I've worked so hard this year as manager. And I've really tried to help the cheerleaders out too. Like the time I spent all night sewing on your uniforms." Hillary could really talk, so on she went. "And now I've worked so hard on this homecoming dance." She talked on, and melted the hearts of Sally, Suzie, Buffy and Sandy. When Hillary finished rehearsing, each cheerleader was almost crying.

"I'm not voting for Hillary!" Bill, the team captain, said. It was later that night at the dance.

"Why not?" Sally questioned.

"Hillary has been an okay manager, but she's not homecoming queen material." Bill was thinking what the whole football team was thinking. Hillary, queen? Besides her physical characteristics not fitting the traditional mold of a homecoming queen, she was brash, forceful and used her Miss Piggy-type personality to push through what she wanted. Such a personality has a tendency to rub high school boys the wrong way.

"What do you mean by that?" asked Sally. "Look at this great dance. She practically did it herself. And she's been nice to the cheerleaders as well. Listen, Bill, if you want me to be happy, you'll vote for Hillary. And you know I'm a lot nicer when I'm happy."

"Okay, okay," Bill answered, shaking his head.

"Good. Now go get the rest of the team to vote for her." Sally was really twisting the knife.

"What?" Bill was dying now.

Similar conversations were going on all over the dance floor. The cheerleaders bribed, begged and stole votes for Hillary. I've never seen a more effective campaign waged on the high school level. When the vote was counted, Hillary was Homer's first homecoming queen, much to the disapproval of the football players.

Years have passed and I'm not sure where Hillary is, but I wouldn't be surprised wherever she is. In fact, I'll bet if she's not president of the United States, she's probably his wife and running things anyway.

Another notable event was that the advisory school board voted football to become a school-sponsored sport. So beginning the next fall, football was in at the high school with a regular varsity schedule.

Chapter 56

Wrestling season began. Wrestling is one of the oldest sports in the history of the world. Wrestlers participating in the sport are carved in the stone of Egyptian antiquity. Interestingly, the moves and holds the Egyptians were using as depicted by the 6,000-year-old carvings are the same moves and holds taught and used today. The human body has changed little in the last 6,000 years.

Wrestling is a unique sport in that it fosters individualism like no other. Wrestling develops in a young boy the rugged individualism that has made America great throughout history.

Nowadays community and business leaders are asking educators to teach students to be team players, or how to work together as a team. However, the business and community teams that I have felt worked together best were those where every individual did his job and one person didn't have to do the job of another team member because he wouldn't or didn't do his job. Wrestling develops people who do their jobs. If I were a general in the Army I'd want soldiers who were wrestlers, because I'd know that they'd do their job even if everyone around them was falling apart.

Wrestling not only develops character, it develops characters. One of the team's characters that year was Eric Peters. Eric was a good wrestler, smart, athletic, but I would say not focused, especially when it came to grades. He would have been a champion if he had kept his grades up so he could have stayed on the team. His chief contribution to the team, besides a win or two, was at the supermarket.

I usually took the team to a supermarket before returning home. Those 250-mile trips were tolerable for wrestlers only if they had something to munch on. Eric loved supermarkets. As far as he was concerned, they were more entertaining than a circus.

His favorite trick was to find gourmet or extremely unusual food items like caviar or pickled pigs feet and then secretly slip them in the basket of some unsuspecting shopper. Then he would wait at the checkout stand with a big smirk on his face and enjoy the reaction as the shopper came to check out their food.

I learned about this antic later in the season when Eric was no longer on the team. His grades had caught up with him and he was academically ineligible to participate in sports. Some of the team members related the whole thing to me.

"Oh, no," I said. "What did the people do?"

"Most of them got mad at the cashier and yelled a lot, but some looked embarrassed and went ahead and bought the things anyway," the team told me.

Twice I had to take action against Eric. Once he scared a lady in the store by acting like he was going to attack her with a salami. And another time I delayed our return for over an hour while I made him scrape up cheese from the floor of one supermarket. He had bought a brick of cheese and then hid behind stacks of cans, aisles, etc., and bombarded shoppers from his hiding place with cheese balls.

I think the teachers eventually were unhappy they made him ineligible. Eric's philosophy was "Don't get mad, get even," and so he did. After he was ineligible he spent the next two weeks in the school library after school. The teachers thought he had really turned the corner and was studying hard, but not Eric. Eric was looking through the school magazines and clipping out the "Send no money now" advertisements. He then filled in the names and addresses of his various teachers and a few of the students he didn't like. In about two weeks several kids and nearly every teacher received literally hundreds of bras, panty hose, *Playboy* magazines and other items they didn't want. Of course, all were expected to pay for them. It was a long time before that mess got straightened out. Eric had long since moved out of the school before anyone found out who did it. I've often wondered which prison Eric ended up in.

Leon Brownson, our heavyweight, was suave and debonair ... at least for a heavyweight. He had eaten at Denny's and other fine restaurants, and so when Jesse Day showed what a country bumpkin he was at breakfast, Leon had to make fun of him all day.

"How would you like your eggs?" the waitress asked.

"Cooked," drawled Jesse.

"Cooked? Cooked? Ha, ha. Jesse says he wants his eggs cooked!" Leon guffawed and the whole team laughed with Leon.

When things settled a little bit, I said, "Over-easy, Jesse. Tell her, over-easy."

"Over-easy," Jesse said, but he was beet red with embarrassment.

I was suspicious a lot of the other boys didn't know how to order eggs either because when asked, every one of them said, "Over-easy."

We had a great day wrestling that day. We had beaten four small-school teams. Two teams even combined their teams to wrestle us and we beat them 57-13. It looked like no Division II (our division) team could touch us. The kids wanted to celebrate.

"Let's go get a steak," someone said.

"No doubt."

"Cosmic."

"Decent."

"Right on."

"Crackerjack."

Every team member had his own catch phrase of agreement this year. To everyone's frustration (but their own), they used it on everything.

"Let's go to the Black Angus."

"No doubt."

"Cosmic."

"Decent."

"Right on."

"Crackerjack."

So we found ourselves at the Black Angus steak house. Leon, suave as always, asked the waiter for a menu and very chicly snapped his fingers when he was ready to order. I could see the entire team was impressed. He could see that as well.

"I would like a Number Five," he said, lowering his voice so he'd sound older.

"A New York. A fine choice," said the waiter. "How would you like it done?"

"Over-easy," said Leon.

"Over-easy?" said the waiter.

"Over-easy!" I said.

Leon dropped his head in his hands. "I can't believe I said that."

The rest of the team caught on and all hee-hawed, followed by a chorus of "No doubt, Cosmic, Decent, Right on, Crackerjack."

At the Seward tournament Steele Jones, the coach for Palmer, showed his character. The referees, especially one old referee, would not call illegal holds. They were so uninformed about what was illegal that to prevent injury to one of my wrestlers' opponents, I ran out on the mat to stop the dangerous situation. (This was not a socially acceptable thing for a wrestling coach to do.) All the coaches recognized the problem and in the coaches' room several expressed fear for their wrestlers' well-being. Steele spoke up:

"I think it's time for a lecture. Let's get the referees and coaches together."

None of us knew what was going to happen, but we knew Steele and we knew something very interesting would ensue. We met with the referees on the mat between rounds of wrestling. Steele spoke to Bill, the most uninformed of the referees.

"Do you know what a Princeton is?"

No, Bill didn't know what a Princeton was.

"This is a Princeton," and Steele trussed Bill's arms up above his head. The Princeton stretches out the neck and shoulder muscles into a very painful position. It also shuts off the air pipe, making breathing very difficult.

Bill screamed until his wind was shut off to a slow gurgle. Then Steele began his lecture on illegal, painful and potentially dangerous holds. All the time Bill gurgled quietly in Steele's Princeton hold. Steele covered the subject very well and I believe was very effective. Bill (after he was able to get his arms and neck back in normal position) refereed much better the rest of the tournament.

Chapter 57

Our young wrestling team (mostly sophomores and some very good freshmen) was anchored by some very tough veterans. We were tearing up the wrestling world. At least I thought we were. Division I wrestling teams (those above 400 students) were definitely giving us trouble. We were able to beat several Division I teams in our region, but just barely. Others, like Kenai, thoroughly trounced us.

Three things made me feel good as the coach. One, the boys kept improving as the year went along. They began beating wrestlers who had beat them previously. I believe it was because they were young, learned quickly and Coach Poindexter had them in such excellent condition, which also contributed to the second thing that made me feel good. They never quit wrestling until the last whistle. They wrestled hard and never gave up if they were behind and never let the pressure off if they were ahead. Wrestlers like that make coaching a joy. Third, we soundly trounced everyone in our division.

Seward, who felt they had the best team in years, we easily beat 38-13. Cordova and another team in our region combined their team with Seldovia, and we still beat them 57-13. To be challenged, we had to wrestle Division I schools, which had as many as 3,000 students compared to our 300 or so. We even won a few dual matches against the big guys, but this year Division I was very tough, and occasionally we got beaten pretty soundly. However, I took pride in the fact that each time we wrestled a team we did better than the previous time.

I wanted to really test the boys against other Division II teams, so I accepted an invitation from Barrow High School who offered to fly us in to wrestle them if we would travel to Fairbanks. It was a long trip, but it gave us a chance to wrestle Eielsen and Delta, two other very tough teams in our division.

Our van trip to Fairbanks was an exercise in patience. The catch phrases of each wrestler I must have heard 1,000 times. Conversation went like this:

"Only 200 more miles to Delta."

"No doubt."

"Cosmic."

"Decent."

"Right on."

"Crackerjack."

"Where we staying at, Coach?"

"In Delta High School."
"No doubt."
"Cosmic."
"Decent."
"Right on."
"Crackerjack."
"Hey, only 180 miles to go."
"No doubt."
"Cosmic."
"Decent."
"Right on."
"Crackerjack."

After much patience we made it to Delta High School, where we had the three-way match with Delta and Eielsen. Delta was a farm community school in the interior of Alaska, and Eielsen was a military school associated with Eielsen Air Force Base near Fairbanks. Both were Division II schools and supposed to be pretty good wrestling teams. Eielsen was the defending state Division II champion and undefeated this year. Delta was the only team in the area that could challenge them. This would be a good test for our team.

I really enjoyed these small three-way matches. The small ones are run on one mat. Each team sits on one group of chairs which are set up on one of the sides of the mat, with the fourth side being reserved for the score table. At the first weight class, Team A's 98-pounder wrestles Team B's 98-pounder, and team C would get a bye. Then at the 103 weight class, Team B would wrestle Team C, and Team A would get the bye. The match would continue through the weight classes three times, with all wrestlers wrestling two opponents. It was intensely fun. Wrestlers from three teams, the crowd, and all the coaches yelled out encouragement and help. A three-way match on one mat takes a long time (sometimes hours), but it was fun to get to concentrate on each and every match and to be so focused. For coaches it was a night to get hoarse, but I usually didn't sing in the church choir during wrestling season anyway.

The team score was kept by adding to the total of each team's score as the match happened, through the entire three rounds. The scores often got to be quite large, 101-96-15 for example.

Homer was the first to come out on the mat and warm up. Homer had a reserved warm-up: a few calisthenics, stretching exercises, and a rather quiet performance. Then out came Eielsen dressed in red and black, hoods pulled down over their eyes. They came out ringing cow bells, shouting, doing drop-steps, cariocas, and other fancy steps and looking pretty scary or silly, depending on your point of view. After Eielsen's performance, Delta did their warm-up chanting, "One, two, three, Delta!" on every exercise. Each wrestler was sizing up his opponent, watching his every move, trying to guess how it would be to wrestle him.

The pre-match ceremony is an intense time for wrestlers. They are looking at that opponent, aware their opponents are looking at them. Like a flock of peacocks, they strut, flex and put on a show for each other. In reality, how an opponent looks has little to do with how tough he is. Some of the toughest-looking wrestlers are easily beaten and some of the wimpiest-looking are the toughest men in the gym, but in pre-match warm-ups, you can never convince high school boys of that.

So, all the strutting and parading comes to a halt as the teams and each individual wrestlers are introduced by weight class. The three opponents come to the center and shake hands. Each wrestler's handshake is part of "psyching out" his opponent. Some stare them down, some won't even look at their opponent, some won't shake at all, but just slap their opponent's hands away. Some try to give a bone-crusher shake to impress their opponent with their strength.

Lane Zeller, a former college teammate of mine, used to give his opponent a limp handshake and say, in the most effeminate manner he could, "Hi, my name is Lane. Shall we play?" Most of his opponents did not want to ever touch him after that introduction. Lane was a great wrestler who knew how to take advantage of that situation and was a consistent winner.

I loved to see Newby Ormsby go out and shake hands. He had a big smile glued on his face. Then, in penguin fashion, a perfect imitation of Charlie Chaplin, he waddled out to shake hands. All the stares and hard handshakes seemed to melt away when he came to the center of the mat.

And so we began wrestling. In the first round the Homer boys were a little lethargic from traveling such a long way, and they made a few mistakes, but they held their own. At the end of the first round the score read: Eielsen 43, Homer 42, Delta 29. The second round began and the lethargy left as Homer pounded each opponent. Both Eielsen and Delta had tough wrestlers, but in most matches Homer was the winner. The second-round score: Homer 98, Eielsen 69, Delta 49. The third round came and, to my surprise, even though Homer kept winning, Eielsen picked up some forfeits and a few pins against Delta, and they began to catch us. Their team saw the score creep closer: Homer 110, Eielsen 84; Homer 113, Eielsen 96; Homer 120, Eielsen 115.

And now was the heavyweight final match, Peter Beneboe of Homer versus Giles Hagoth from Eielsen. Peter was a heavyweight who looked a lot younger than his years. He looked soft, easy to handle. His opponent was a tad heavier than him and a head shorter, but he had big biceps, strong legs and shoulders. From first observation it appeared as if Eielsen had this match in the bag, but underneath Peter's soft exterior was smooth, flexible muscle and a heart of gold. He listened to everything that the coaches taught. He ran, he did calisthenics right along with the rest of the team. Quite often a heavyweight is not able to keep up with the rest of the team in the conditioning tasks of practice, but Peter did. With effort, but without complaint. Peter had also developed a Fireman's Carry, a very unusual move for a heavyweight to have in his repertoire of takedowns. Peter was able to use his Fireman's Carry to not only take his opponents down to the mat, but also to put them on their backs in pinning position.

And so the two heavyweights stepped to the center of the mat. If the Eielsen boy pinned Peter, Eielsen would win. If anything else happened, Homer would win. The crowd (pro-Eielsen and Delta) cheered wildly as Hagoth stepped onto the mat. They were sure this was going to be a pin for Eielsen. James Davis, the Eielsen coach, holding a printed program in his hand, had just finished his pep talk with a slap of the program on the shoulder. The scowl on the coach's face and the hard intensity of his stance all portrayed a man who felt this was an important, even crucial, time.

My pep talk to Peter consisted of: "Peter, do your best and wrestle this match like any other you've wrestled. The man is just another opponent." Peter nodded, never spoke a word, and strode to the center.

The wrestlers shook hands at the center, the referee blew the whistle and Hagoth attacked immediately. Peter dropped in under him, picked up an arm and leg, used Hagoth's forward motion to beautifully wheel him across his shoulders in perfect Fireman's position and right to his back. Hagoth was so surprised his mouth came open. Peter used the moment's delay in his reaction to secure him on his back and tighten his grip. The referee was down on the mat looking at Hagoth's shoulders. Hagoth struggled in one direction, then the other. Peter, in bulldog fashion, tightened his grip with each struggle. Soon both Hagoth's shoulders were in contact with the mat. The referee counted, "One, two," and slapped the mat. Peter had pinned his opponent.

He jumped up and, after the formal handshake, bounced his way back to his team in celebration. Homer had won! Homer 126, Eielsen 115, Delta 53. We had beat the defending state champs, the supposedly best team in the state. I looked across the mat. Coach Davis just hit his hand with his rolled-up program over and over again in frustration.

After that great win against two recognized great opponents, the rest of the trip was almost an anticlimax. The trip to Barrow, where we wrestled two dual meets, was routine. Barrow High School at times had outstanding wrestling teams. My first few years my wrestlers took Barrow for granted and sometimes were very much surprised by some very strong Eskimo wrestlers who soon had them fighting to keep their backs off the mat. However, this year, in the two days of wrestling, we only lost one individual match.

While in Barrow, the team did learn about some of the interesting cultural aspects of a town that far north. Only two buildings in Barrow were hooked up to the sewer system — the high school and the hospital. No other dwellings had a sewer system. This was partly because of the permafrost which is permanently frozen soil below a depth of about one foot. The permafrost would freeze all underground sewer pipes without an elaborate heating system. Also, the sewer treatment plant was so new that few had had time to hook up if they could. So most of the townspeople still used indoor "honey pots." In Europe they are called "chamber pots." I'm not sure what the Barrow citizens did with the contents when full.

The houses all had gas heat for free. This was not a government give-away program. A few years earlier someone discovered that if you drove a pipe into the ground a few feet you had natural gas, so nearly everyone did and had warm cozy gas heat all year long. A few still survived the winter in the old-fashioned way with old smudge pots and "parkas."

The Eskimo parka is an invention of necessity, but has worked very well for these people for thousands of years. A real parka is nearly floor-length and covers the person from head to toe like a large heavy dress. When temperatures get quite low, -40 to -50 degrees Fahrenheit (it stayed colder than -40 degrees our entire trip), the Eskimo puts on another parka over his first parka to get a good layered effect.

With a parka and good thick fur boots called "mukluks," the Eskimo is ready for any weather. When Eskimo hunters are traveling and their feet get cold, they fold the parka around their feet and set down on them until they warm up and then continue the hunt. It is really quite amazing that these people were able to adapt so well to such a harsh environment.

The traditional Eskimos did not change their underclothing. Nor did they change parkas or bathe for the entire winter. With temperatures that low, it would be unwise to change without a good heat source. Most of the people in Barrow at this time do not live in the old-fashioned way. With natural gas as their heat source, they live much as other Alaskans, but a few still live as they have for thousands of years. However, these traditional Eskimos are not popular in public places; they do have a unique odor after wearing the same clothes for six months.

The weather was cold with a strong wind making it even colder. It was hard for us south-Alaskans to go outside, but I did take the team to the farthest north point in Alaska. It was a little hard to tell where the land ended and the ice pack began, but a local resident showed us the spot. Of course, the kids had to run out on the ice pack and look for seal holes and polar bears and other semi-mythical stuff. Somehow in the -40 temperatures they managed to have fun. Later they braved the wind to walk down about 10 blocks to the only grocery store in town to buy snacks. Why they wanted to buy snacks in the most expensive spot in America, I'll never know. However, I should have remembered that, after all, when wrestlers are not cutting weight, they're snacking. The next morning mysteriously all the snacks had disappeared overnight. After the season I found out that Newby Ormsby, Dave Scalzi and Eugene Ukulele had raided everyone's snacks and ate everything. I wondered why they were all eight pounds over the next Monday.

Chapter 58

In every season it seems there are extreme highs and lows. Every coach tries to figure out how to make his extreme high at the end of the season. We had a good high, but now came the long slope to a discouraging low. Eugene Ukulele got in trouble with grades and became ineligible in English. Bob Stonum and Heath Smith quit because they were afraid their grades were going down. Dave Scalzi couldn't keep his weight down, so he went up to a weight class and beat his cousin Newby Ormsby out at that weight, eliminating one very good wrestler who could have helped us in the regional tournament. Peter Beneboe injured his knee. Vance Long, a freshman, broke his leg. His dad vowed that he would never let him wrestle again. Leon Brownson's dad died in a fishing accident. Leon was never the same after that and eventually dropped out of wrestling completely. Jason Hill left to go fishing and the straw that broke the camel's back, Doug Scalzi, our undefeated senior, separated his shoulder in a match with Kenai. The doctor felt it was doubtful he could wrestle the rest of the year. Doug's dad flew him to Anchorage for a specialist to look him over. The specialist said that if he did not use it until regionals, he might be able to wrestle. So with a sadly depleted team, we dropped three dual matches to Soldotna, Palmer and Wasilla.

The young kids still stuck in there though. We had good hard practices, and slowly things improved. Heath Smith and Bob Stonum asked to come back on the team, and everyone kept getting better. We had a freshman, aptly named Matt Quick, who filled in at the 98-pound weight class which Dave Scalzi had vacated, and he began beating other good varsity wrestlers. A little chubby-looking sophomore, Stan Gear, moved up to wrestle heavyweight and turned into an animal. Issac Newgate, a freshman, had an even record, but then began winning and won his last four matches. Not everyone was back, but the team pulled together and once again we felt like a team. We had one final match before regionals — Bethel. Bethel was also undefeated against Division II schools and they were coming to Homer for a dual match just before they went to their regionals. This would be a good tune-up for our regionals as well.

The night of the Bethel match came. The stands were filled. Nina brought the whole family. It was the custom for the little kids to go out on the mat just prior to the teams coming in for warm-up. The kids ran around, chased each other, played tag and some even wrestled. Rebekah happened to be standing on the mat when a little boy just younger than she walked stiff-legged towards her. He had just learned to walk and was rocking from side to side as he made his way across the mat, arms out in front, Frankenstein-style. He wobbled right up to Becky, put his arms around her and before she knew it, kissed her on the cheek. Only after the kiss did she realize what was happening. She screamed, pushed the boy away and ran to her mother. The poor boy had fallen to his seat and with wide eyes looked around as if to say, "What did I do wrong?" For him that was a delicate age to be introduced to how all of us men feel most of the time when dealing with women.

Bethel was a pretty tough team, but when Homer stepped on the mat with hundreds of fans cheering, screaming and calling out advice, the Homer cream came to the top. Homer won every match but one. Doug Scalzi's replacement had put up a good fight, but had lost by a few points. Every match was determined by a decision indicating that the teams were much closer then the score indicated. The final team score was Homer 31, Bethel 3.

Ron Geoble, the Bethel coach, was devastated. He came over and shook hands with me and congratulated our fine team. He seemed embarrassed, but I continued the conversation with him. I talked about his fine wrestlers and how each had done and how impressed I was with some of their wrestling. He warmed up right away and we parted on very good terms. I was very pleased. This was an excellent thing to happen before the regional tournament. The team knew they were the best Division II team in the state. They had beaten every team that was supposed to be good and they had done it soundly. Even more good news came that evening. The doctor had declared Doug Scalzi healed and ready to wrestle. One week was not a lot of time to get in shape or come back to top wrestling form, but I knew if anyone could do it, Doug could.

Wrestling practice was intense that week. We had drills, lots of wrestling, and an extra half-hour of practice to run sprints. Wrestling practice is the most grueling of all sports practices. I've had wrestlers who also were in cross-country running, skiing, hockey, basketball, football, each were in excellent shape and each was exhausted after as little as an hour of practice.

One day a well-muscled basketball player came into practice and said that wrestling practice didn't look that tough. I had him wrestle Isaac Newgate, a freshman about his size, who pounded on him and pushed him and rolled him around the mat until he begged for mercy he was so tired. About that time Dave Scalzi, one of our smallest wrestlers, jumped on his back, grabbed the back of his shirt, dug his heels into the basketball boy's sides and yelled, "Yee haw, ride 'em cowboy!" The poor fellow was so tired he couldn't respond even to that humiliation.

Wrestling practice usually begins with some slow running or jogging for 20 minutes to warm up, followed by a multitude of stretching exercises. A wrestler has to be not only strong, but flexible. Flexibility prevents injuries, so we take stretching very seriously. There is a series of yoga stretches we do in complete silence, with everyone concentrating and only the team captain calling out when the change to the next exercise.

Then it's time for instruction. During instruction time every aspect of wrestling must be covered. As many matches as each wrestler wrestles, it is likely that one or several will see each situation. I've found that to be a good wrestling coach one must be a master teacher and follow most of the techniques a good teacher uses when he teaches any subject.

To teach a new move or technique in wrestling, I do the following: I demonstrate the move in its entirety, then I break it down into parts and explain why each part must be done in that certain way. The next phase is to put wrestlers with partners and have each of the partners go through the move as I prompt them in what they should do during each part of the move. I then have them repeat, doing the same move with me giving fewer prompts. I continue to do this until the wrestlers are doing the move correctly without prompts. The next few days I review the move with the wrestlers and then add it to our drill routine.

Drilling is the next part of practice. Drilling at the beginning of the year is the most challenging part of practice. However, as the season progresses and as the team truly learns the moves and is able to do them immediately as the coach calls them out, the drilling part of practice looks like a ballet. Every wrestler is in unison, stepping, ducking, falling, throwing and moving as one well-oiled machine. A team that has learned its moves and drills them well is truly beautiful to behold.

During college I once took a girl to a wrestling match. Her comment to me after a few matches shocked me.
She said, "I wish they were all nude." She was an artist and she explained that to see so many powerful muscles in motion was an artist's dream. I can understand how she felt when I see a well-schooled team drilling wrestling moves in unison. It is power in motion. I've never wished they were nude however.

Drilling is a fairly exhausting part of practice, but what follows is where the conditioning comes in. Practice now turns to wrestling.

Usually everyone in the room is wrestling with a partner, and wrestling is exhausting. Not only are you pushing and pulling a weight the same as yours through some very difficult maneuvers, that weight is actively trying to keep you from doing it and at the same time trying to push you or pull you through other maneuvers. A six-minute match is more than the average man can last. To get a wrestler in top shape, however, he may wrestle three to eight regular six-minute matches during a practice. A person has to be well-conditioned to do that, but young men learn to do it and learn to do it easily.

Finally, wrestling practice concludes with some conditioning calisthenics. A wrestler who pushes himself through such a practice usually has very little fat on his body. His muscularity is well-defined and he is a man in terrific shape. I think no human being gets in better overall body shape than a well-conditioned wrestler. Of course, as I mentioned, to prepare for regionals we added a half-hour of sprints to practice to get them in really good shape. The kids worked hard and both Coach Poindexter and I knew they were ready for regionals.

Chapter 59

Nothing chills you to the bone like a late March night in Soldotna, Alaska. Especially with wind and sleet mixed with rain gnawing at every crack in your clothing. Soldotna is always a little colder than Homer for some reason, but tonight it was particularly cold as I walked from the regional seeding meeting to the church where the Homer team was sleeping. I believe it was particularly cold because I realized how stupid I was.

I hadn't been feeling particularly chipper when I went to the meeting. I was sweating more than usual and had a headache, but I put on my best poker face and stepped into the seeding meeting.

The regional seeding meeting is perhaps the most fun day of the wrestling coach's year. It is like playing a giant poker game where the stakes are maneuvering your wrestler in each weight class to the position on the bracket that is best for him. Coaches use their statistics, win-loss records, and their wiles to jockey their wrestlers into the best position and yet also jockey other teams' wrestlers into positions of disadvantage. Usually, even with inexperience, I've done well in these seeding meetings, but tonight nearly everything went wrong.

Somehow the other coaches wouldn't believe me when I explained how much my wrestlers had improved through the year. Everyone I put up for seeding was seeded either fourth or fifth. Fifth place was just as bad as fourth; it meant that each boy would have to wrestle the first-seeded wrestler before finals. I really felt that many of our boys had a real shot at beating the second-seeded wrestler, but the first-place wrestler was unbeatable. Weight class after weight class came and one after another of the Homer wrestlers were seeded fourth or fifth. The harder I tried to convince people of the potential of my wrestlers, the harder the other coaches stuck to the fact that earlier in the season Homer wrestlers had lost to someone who was also in the tournament.

At Doug Scalzi's weight class it looked like they would seed this undefeated wrestler fourth also, because of his long absence with injury. I said in disgust, "Just draw him in. It doesn't matter. He'll beat anyone in the tournament so it doesn't matter where he is, so just draw him in."

Suddenly everyone took me seriously and finally seeded him second, even though he'd beaten the person who was seeded first. Somehow it seemed it was one of those nights that I was going to lose every poker hand. So in a dark mood I trudged through the dark night with the dark news.

I had made copies of the seeding for my whole team and I passed them out and let them look it over before I gave my "I'm sorry" speech. They looked the seeding over and almost in unison shouted, "This is great, I got seeded fourth. Great job, Coach." I thought at first they were being sarcastic, but they were truly pleased.

"Coach, how did you get me seeded ahead of Jones?" and other comments such as that turned my dark mood into an almost festive one. After the excited discussions died down, the kids all checked their weight on the portable scales we had, and those who could afford it drank a Gatorade in celebration.

The next day I woke up really sick. I was stiff and sore all over. My stomach was doing flip-flops. The sweat was rolling off my forehead and over my brows like a waterfall one minute and the next I'd be shivering so hard that a blanket couldn't keep me warm. I used my secret weapon for colds, and flu, Alka-Seltzer Cold Plus, but even that old faithful failed to touch this illness. I was able to crawl to the van and somehow with help, I got the kids to the tournament. It was a good thing Al Poindexter was there. He could handle the team pretty well by himself, but this illness had taken away two of my most useful coaching weapons.

During a wrestling match, a coach cannot call time-out to coach his wrestlers, but he is allowed to coach and shout instructions from his chair on the side of the mat. This was a great advantage for me, because I have a loud voice. My voice is often so loud that wrestlers say they can hear me clear across a noisy gym when they could hear nobody else. I also have wrestled so much that I could feel what should be done by each of my wrestlers in every situation. This is a great advantage for the beginning wrestler especially. Today, however, I couldn't feel anything except a pounding head. My voice was gone, so I couldn't shout anything. I wasn't much help to the wrestlers for both days of the tournament. I sat hunched over with a large coat and hat. Sometimes I even made it to the side of the mat, but I never had the strength to even open my mouth.

The first day the kids didn't seem to miss me. Our first round, in the first 12 matches, we picked up 12 pins. We had 36 points, well ahead of Kenai at 27, or any other team in the tournament. In the second round we had eight more wins which put eight of our guys in the semi-final matches. I was awake enough to remember several coaches' comments to me that I had been right in the seeding meeting — my kids had improved greatly. It was hard not to remember these comments, because all the coaches, after seeing how bad I looked, shouted their comments from well out of contagious range.

From that point on however, like a falling star trailing clouds of glory, the Homer team fell. It is not fair to indicate that the team fell apart. The team wrestled with the hearts of badgers. But they also wrestled against the very best competition in the state and it was tough for men, young and inexperienced as they were, to dominate as they had previously.

Jesse Day, a sophomore who had previously never placed in a tournament, took on the returning state champion Kevan Buyers. Kevan was so good that he didn't condition and it was obvious in his match with Jesse. In fact he had to cheat to win.

Kevan was the undefeated state champ and looked every bit of it as he stepped on the mat. He was long and lean, with a well-muscled upper body and sturdy, but wiry, legs. He had sharp blue eyes, a handsome angular face with a shock of blond hair. He stepped on the mat with a cocky, jaunty step that said, "This is going to be easy." Jesse on the other hand looked like the farm kid he was: hard-knotted muscles, goofy face with a ready ear-to-ear smile. Jesse's face and timid stride said, "I'm just glad to be here."

This was a semi-final match. The winner went to finals and thus on to the state championships. The loser was an also-ran.

Kevan had easily pinned Jesse earlier in the year and as the match began, it looked like a repeat of the previous match. Within seconds Kevan had Jesse taken down and on his back. Jesse struggled and fought, never allowing Kevan to quite get both shoulders down, and finally struggled out of his dangerous position. Then Jesse continued to fight for an escape. Kevan eventually just let him go. The almost identical scene ensued. Jesse was on his back and again, no matter what Kevan did, Jesse kept at least one shoulder up and eventually struggled free. Again Kevan let him go just before the end of the round, and Kevan was visibly fatigued.

Kevan was very slow to come to the center for the coin toss. He won the coin toss and so chose down position for the second round. The score was now 10-2. The wrestling had been so straightforward that there should have been no question as to the score, but Kevan asked the referee to check the score anyway, thus stretching the time between rounds to almost two minutes, giving him some rest that he badly needed.

On the whistle Kevan executed a beautiful standing switch; he lifted Jesse's near leg, stepped between Jesse's legs and hooked him by the head to tilt him right to his back. Jesse was now down 15-2, but with a heart as big as the universe, Jesse fought off his back and kept the motion up. With Herculean effort, Jesse reversed an extremely tired Buyers who dropped his head just enough for Jesse to also slap in a cradle. Now Kevan was on his back fighting for his life. A cradle is a very dangerous move. It is not dangerous to the wrestler's health, only to his ego, because it is so hard to prevent being pinned in one. It is a well-known fact in college circles that a really good wrestler cannot be pinned, except with a cradle. And now Jesse Day, farm kid from Homer, down 15-4, had the returning state champion on his back in a cradle. And those farm boy hands that had milked cows every day for many years were not going to let go.

Suddenly the gym resounded with an ear-splitting wail coming from Kevan. The referee blew the whistle, stopping the match. Kevan grabbed his knee and wriggled on the mat in agony. My first thought was, "He must have dislocated his knee." My second thought was, "How could he hurt his knee in a cradle?"

Kevan was attended by his coach who immediately called for the paramedics, but Kevan said no, and waved them away while he continued to massage his right knee for almost the full two minutes of allowed recovery time. He suddenly stood and strode to the center of the mat without a limp. He glanced at the score which now read 15-7, still in his favor, 17 seconds left in the second round. Kevan now looked well-rested. He easily knelt down on both knees to take his bottom starting position. In wrestling, when the match is stopped for any reason, it is re-started in referee's position. Jesse would have loved to re-start the match as it had stopped, with him locked up on a cradle and his opponent on his back. Now his opponent was starting on hands and knees, a much more advantageous position for Kevan, not for Jesse.

The referee blew the whistle. In a matter of seconds Kevan reversed Jesse and had him on his back and the round ended. Score 20-7. I couldn't stand it. I got up in my weakened condition and walked behind the coaches' chairs, walked back and forth. It was obvious Kevan had faked an injury to prevent being pinned, but I could do nothing about it. I finally turned to Jesse and shouted, "Jesse, take top and go for the pin. Jesse, don't quit! Don't quit! He's tired, you can beat him! Keep the pressure on!"

Jesse grinned at me. He was not discouraged; in fact, regardless of the score, he was having fun. Kevan's head, on the other hand, was low, his chest was heaving and his skin was flushed.

Because Jesse chose top position, Kevan had down position in the last round also. He took as long as he could in getting in down position. He was experienced at stalling. Stalling is illegal in wrestling. A wrestler must wrestle aggressively at all times and from all positions. However, with two minutes to go in the match and being as tired as this Homer farm boy had made him, the only thing he could do was stall. Regardless of the rules, this is just what Kevan did. He slowly put one knee down at a time. Slowly shook one hand, put it down. He shook the other hand and put it down. He raised his right leg and shook it, put it down slowly, then he raised the other leg and shook it slowly, then put it down. Another minute of rest Kevan had stalled out. This kind of activity puts a referee in a hard position. He must make a judgment call that the boy is stalling when he is doing things other wrestlers often do, just not quite so slowly or so much. This referee chose not to call stalling at this time.

Jesse immediately got into his top position. The whistle started the last round. Kevan stiffened his arms and sat on his haunches, mule-like. He bowed his back and would not let Jesse move him. For 30 seconds Jesse used every ploy to move him. The referee yelled out, "Warning — stalling, Soldotna."

The match continued. Kevan went to his belly and stiffened his legs and arms, spreading them out and arching his back. Again Jesse could not move him.

"Stalling, Soldotna, one point Homer," the referee yelled. The score was now 20-8.

Kevan rose to his knees and then went to his belly. More movement, but the referee was not fooled. Ten seconds later he yelled, "Stalling, Soldotna, two points Homer." The score was now 20-10, but more importantly, if Kevan was called for stalling one more time he would automatically be disqualified and lose the match. However, he had stalled over a minute; less than a minute was left in the match.

Kevan, with one last burst of strength, reversed Jesse and tried to turn Jesse to his back. But Jesse fought back. He was not going to get turned. For 20 seconds he fought off his Soldotna opponent. Meanwhile Kevan used every bit of his strength. He had nothing left at all. Jesse executed the one switch he knew and easily picked up a cradle on the exhausted Buyers. Now Jesse had Buyers on his back, but the score was 22-12. A near-fall would only give Jesse three points. Jesse had to pin. Jesse maneuvered Kevan, who was as pliable as clay, to his back. Kevan struggled once, twice, then screamed in pretended pain. The referee blew the whistle, stopping the match. Kevan was now holding the other knee as if in pain. I knew he was faking, the referee knew he was faking, his coach (looking a little embarrassed) knew he was faking. But there was little anyone could do about it. I had completely exhausted myself saying the few words I had to Jesse, but Al ran right over to the timekeeper and asked how much injury time Buyers had.

"Fifteen seconds," was the reply.

"Well, start the watch," Al said.

"Oh, okay," said the timekeeper (who had not yet started the injury time), a bit embarrassed. Fifteen seconds was completed, Buyers had to wrestle now or forfeit. He crawled to the center. Twelve seconds were left in the match. The score was 22-15 in favor of the Soldotna boy.

The match began again. Again Jesse cradled Buyers and after a small struggle Buyers was again on his back with five seconds left in the match. It only takes two seconds to pin a wrestler, but Kevan Buyers was too experienced to be pinned that quickly and he kept one shoulder up until the match ended. Final score 22-18, Buyers had won.

Kevan Buyers crawled to the center, stood on shaky legs and let the referee raise his hand. Jesse strode from the center. "Jesse," I said, "they raised the other guy's hand, but you were the winner out there." Jesse's face lit up like a Christmas tree. "Thanks. Can I have a drink of Gatorade, Coach?"

"Sure, Jesse, take as much as you want." I was afraid that he might be really upset at losing in such a manner, but a drink of Gatorade and Jesse was just fine.

Jesse wrestled for the next two years just like that. No one ever doubted that he gave his all and then a little more in every match, but if he lost or if he won, he came off the mat with that big toothy smile and you knew he had fun.

Our third-string sophomore heavyweight became our varsity heavyweight after Peter Beneboe's injury and Leon Brownson dropping out. His name was Stan Gear. Stan had decided he was a "biker." And he had the image — big leather jacket with *Hell's Angels* on the back, biker-type hat (similar to a Greek sailor cap), and even a billfold hooked to his belt by a big long silver chain. He looked like a biker too — grim, unintelligent eyes and gruesome face. He had everything a person needed to be a biker, but a bike. He didn't own a Harley Hog, but everyone thought he must when he dressed like that. They also thought he must be tough. In practice, when I wrestled him, I thought he was sort of a cream puff compared to Doug Scalzi or Jason Hill, but when he wrestled against other teams, beginning with that regional tournament, he scared people. None of his opponents wanted to wrestle "that biker from Homer." And he would wrestle and beat them because they were scared silly of him.

From out of nowhere this unseeded sophomore beat some of the best heavyweights in the region to place third. When he stepped off the mat from his semi-final loss, he said to me, "That will never happen to me again." And it didn't.

Stan eventually did get a bike. He still rides his Harley Hog around town wearing his leather jacket and chain, but I've never known him to ever be belligerent or even get in a fight. He did buy a pitbull because "that's what bikers ought to have." One day I saw Stan walking his dog down the street near my home. I thought it looked funny, this tough-looking biker walking down the street with his dog on a leash. Especially since his dog looked so much like him. What was even funnier was when about a half-hour later Stan came back up the street he was carrying his dog on his shoulder. The dog looked so grateful for not having to walk anymore.

With Jesse, Stan, Dave, Newby and the other young kids doing an outstanding job, we took third in the regional tournament as a team. We had seven third places, but only first- and second-place finishers went to state. Doug Scalzi was our only first-place wrestler. Doug's shoulder had recovered enough to wrestle great, so he waltzed through the tournament. But mainly because of our seeding, no one took second. That meant that Homer, the best Division II school, would go to the state championship with one wrestler, by virtue of the fact that we had to qualify against Division I wrestlers. Regions had really taken their toll. I was too sick at the time to think, but the tournament news made me sicker and yet I couldn't be unhappy with the kids. All had wrestled above their previous best and shown great hearts. I was proud of all of them. I was just sorry these great kids didn't get to go to state.

Chapter 60

Life has a funny way of making bad things turn out good. I try to remember that as much as I can, especially in situations like we were in at that time. I try not to think about the fact that life also sometimes makes good things turn out bad. But that happens too.

I have to admit that this was one of the most discouraging times of my life. Al and I had worked hard for five years building the wrestling program and we knew we had the best wrestling team in the state in the small-schools division, but here we were taking just one wrestler to state.

I had a little catch phrase that I used when things got really discouraging that seemed to help. "Be glad you're discouraged because that means just around the corner the Lord is going to bless you." But it was hard for me to see any blessing coming in this situation. My discouragement prolonged my illness and I was not able to get out of bed until Wednesday. I dragged myself to school, put on my best face and did what a good coach does best — fake enthusiasm.

Al had been practicing Doug the last two days and had him down to weight and in good condition. Doug was one of those naturally well-built individuals with quickness and great athletic ability. Wednesday we fine-tuned his skills and got ready for the long trip to Fairbanks. The state tournament was to be held at the University of Alaska in Fairbanks this year. As far as Homer was concerned, the whole state tournament was now for Doug.

The drive to Fairbanks didn't seem quite so long since we'd already driven it once that year. Still, 700 miles is a long trip. Al Poindexter and Doug were in good spirits, and I caught their mood and only occasionally did I get a bit morose when I thought of all the fine wrestlers on our team who should have been traveling with us.

We pulled in to Patty Gym at the University of Alaska where the tournament was to be held, and headed for the scales to check Doug's weight. Apparently nearly everyone else in the state had the same idea at the same time. Hundreds of boys were stripped down and lined up and checking their weight on the official scales.

One of the first people I saw was Rob Geoble, the Bethel coach. He was happy to see me and we greeted each other with genuine enthusiasm.

"How many boys did you bring?" he asked.

"Only one," I answered with drooped shoulders.

"Oh, that's too bad," he said. He was doing his best to act sympathetic, yet I also felt the glee behind his words.

"It looks like you got a few boys here," I commented.

"Yah, we did okay," he said as he marched 12 Bethel boys by. He had qualified his entire team, the same team we'd beaten 31-3 just a few weeks earlier. Now I was really discouraged.

Doug began the tournament seeded fourth. Which meant he had a rough climb to the top, but the seeding did not discourage him. He easily pinned his first opponent from Metlakatla. His second opponent was Loren Salt from Chugiak. Salt was a long-limbed, tall but wiry wrestler with the heart of a lion. Doug easily out-pointed Salt, but Salt never quit. Doug would take him down, then get bored with trying to turn him over, so he'd let him go and Salt would attack without hesitation. In one of his reckless attacks he rolled his ankle severely. He was in terrible pain, but he told his coach to just fill his shoe with ice. Then back out on the mat as gung-ho as ever he came. Two more takedowns (in one of which Salt had gained control on Doug) went by. Salt was dragging his foot so bad he couldn't put any pressure on it, but he didn't want to quit. His coach threw in the towel which indicated a forfeit and then had to physically drag him off the mat and to the hospital. I learned later that the ankle was severely broken.

Winning that match put Doug in the semi-final, not against the top-seeded wrestler, but against Johnson from Kenai, the same wrestler he had wrestled in the finals of the regional championships. Johnson was a very strong and focused wrestler who had just beaten the number one seed. It took that same kind of focus from Doug to win against Johnson and make it to the finals.

I figured Doug needed to rest and relax and concentrate away from the crowd, so I instructed him to get dressed and we'd go back to the hotel. Coach Poindexter and I got the van to pick him up. He soon came out and got in the van. As we were pulling away, Doug said, "Coach, are you sure the semi-finals are later? I saw Johnson, Massengale and some of the other guys that are in the semi's getting dressed down."

"It says right here in the program, 3:00 p.m. today — semi-finals," Coach Poindexter said.

"Oh, no," I said. "We better check. For something this important it's better safe than sorry." And so I ran back into the gym and checked with the head table official.

"No, the semi's have been changed to this morning starting in about 15 minutes. Didn't you hear the announcement?" was the answer to my question.

"No, we didn't! Maybe you ought to announce it again," I said over my shoulder as I rushed out to the van. Thank goodness for an observant young man, because if we'd have gone back to the hotel we'd have missed the match completely and Doug would have been out of the tournament.

As it was, we had plenty of time for Doug to get ready, get focused and easily out-point Johnson to put himself in the finals against the number two-seeded wrestler, highly touted Massengale from Service High School in Anchorage.

My biggest pet peeve with referees is that some of them, especially those who come from big cities, expect big-city kids to win and so when a small-town boy is winning they think they as referees must be doing something wrong. So they make judgment calls and close calls leaning toward the big-city kid. Not that they're cheating, it's just that they have that orientation. Of course, if I were the referee I'd probably lean the other way.

And so it was with that finals match — a big-city referee refereeing Doug Scalzi, small-town boy, versus big-city Lane Massengale. Lane was every bit as strong as Doug; he was smooth, sleek and an obvious fighting machine. Service High School was a large high school of about 3,000 students. Often they would have 100 boys or more turn out for wrestling. The coach was very smart about handling that number of boys and mostly arranged practices so that they all wrestled each other the entire practice. He spent little time teaching moves or drilling. He taught rules and let them wrestle until the cream came to the top. Service wrestlers were all very unorthodox wrestlers, but very talented. Lane was one of those unorthodox but talented and experienced wrestlers. He faced Doug Scalzi, an orthodox, well-conditioned, well-trained wrestler.

In the first round, both wrestlers started on their feet vying for the takedown. Massengale would shoot for a takedown and Doug would counter the shot in a forceful and proven technique. Doug would shoot a classic takedown and Massengale would scramble, throw legs, arms and hips in all directions until he was free. For 1 minute and 45 seconds this cat-and-mouse game continued, then Doug did what he had been setting up all match. Doug learned from his dad, who was a military man, that a Russian technique of war was to attack a certain point of the enemy line several times and then quickly retreat, making the opponent think that part of the line was strong. Then with a strong force, attack that same place later and break through. Doug adapted this same strategy on Massengale. He weakly attacked the right leg several times and then in the last 15 seconds, with all the technique, strength and quickness he possessed, he attacked that same right leg, surprising and up-ending Massengale for the takedown, just before the end of the first round. Homer 2, Service 0.

Doug started on the bottom the second round and quickly stood up to escape. He fought Lane's hands apart, moved his hips to one side, turned quickly and was facing Massengale, having completed a great classic stand-up escape. Homer 3, Service 0.

About this time the referee began to get worried. "Homer is ahead," he said to himself. "How is that possible? Maybe I'm doing something wrong or I did something wrong." And from that moment he began to call the match from that viewpoint. Not to take anything from either wrestler. Massengale was wrestling like a whirlwind, but Doug was right there as the proverbial lasso on the whirlwind. Close to the end of the second round, Massengale shot hard, straight at Doug. It was a powerful move and took Doug to his hip. Doug countered by scooting his hip away and putting himself in outside switch position, reaching back to put force on Massengale's leg to begin coming out on top. It looked as if Doug was going to get the takedown when both wrestlers scooted off the mat.

"Two points, Green," yelled the referee. For a minute I thought he had given Doug two points a little prematurely. Then I realized we were red.

"What?" I yelled as I jumped to my feet. Times like these, it's hard for a coach not to yell. I stomped over to the score table where the referee met me.

"They were off the mat. No one had control. How can you give a takedown?" I asked as calmly as I could.

"It was a takedown, Coach. Two points, Green."

The rules make it unsportsmanlike to argue with a referee no matter how wrong he is, so all I could do was shrug and stomp back to my chair. Doug was less upset about it than I, so the match continued. The round ended with no change — Doug ahead 3-2.

In the third round Massengale was down. He needed to escape to tie and put the match in overtime. Doug needed to keep him from escaping or to turn him on his back to win. Doug put in his favorite riding hold — a grapevine crossbody. When used right, the crossbody effectively keeps an opponent on the mat and also opens up some fine pinning combinations with exotic names such as guillotine and banana split.

Massengale struggled, Doug held. He struggled more and, like a python, Doug clamped tighter. Nearly half the round continued. Then in sheer frustration, Massengale reached back and grabbed Scalzi's toe on the grapevine leg and reefed on it as hard as he could. Doug screamed in pain. It was clearly an illegal toe-hold. The referee stopped the match. We went to the center, but Doug was okay, it just hurt a little. I looked at the score. Doug had been given no additional point for an illegal hold.

"Is there no penalty point?" I asked the referee.

"No," he answered.

"But a toe-hold is illegal."

"That toe-hold was only potentially dangerous. No points," he said and walked to the center of the mat. The match started again, Massengale jumped to his feet and ran toward the edge of the mat, Doug right behind him. As they went off the mat, the referee blew his whistle and called out, "One point, Green."

Again I went to the score table. "To get an escape the rules clearly say a wrestler must be turned around facing his opponent."

"He would have if they'd not gone off the mat. One point, escape." The score was now tied at 3-3, and so the match ended and overtime began.

In overtime, no points were scored until the third round when Massengale, realizing he could use the toe-hold with this referee, reefed again on Doug's toe. Rather than allow himself to be injured, Doug let Massengale reverse and thus Massengale won the match 5-3. Doug took the loss like a gentleman and we met him at the edge of the mat with open arms and consoling words.

Later, at the award assembly, Doug had received his second-place medal which he was wearing proudly, but it was disappointing. I felt he should have been wearing the gold. They were giving out the team trophies:

"Division II runner-up — Glennallen." Three Glennallen boys walked out to receive their second-place trophy.

"Well, those three sure did great," I said. "Al, I didn't see any of them in the finals. What weight class were they in?"

"The 167-pounder took fourth, but I didn't see any of them in the finals," Al answered.

The announcer continued. "Division II state championship team for 1982 — Homer."

"Homer?" I said.

"Homer?" Al said.

"Homer?" Doug said. "How can you win state with one wrestler?"

"I don't know," I answered, "but you better go get the trophy. You're the only Homer wrestler around."

"Well, what do I do?"

"You just go out there and get that big gold trophy, the one with the wrestler on it. Yah, from the guy who's looking like he doesn't know what to do with it."

Doug went out as red as a beet, but the applause was deafening.

The most improbable thing that could have happened did happen. Homer came to the state tournament with one wrestler, who placed second, and yet took home the state championship team trophy. All other wrestlers in the Division II had been beaten out of the tournament early by Division I wrestlers. Only Doug and the Glennallen boy had earned a place in the tournament. Homer had the best team for Division II all year and then finally won it in the end. I guess that old saying turned out to be true, there was a blessing just around the corner. All things work out in the end if you just stay in there and keep working. Like nothing else ever, that state tournament was a lesson in the fact that discouragement is a stepping stone to success.

We had our Homer wrestling awards banquet a few weeks later. All the wrestlers were there. We'd given out all the awards like "ugliest wrestler," "most likely to survive," etc. when I stood up to give my speech. I gave them a history of wrestling at Homer since Al and I had coached, and talked of the progress they'd made. I talked about how good a team they were. I talked about the discouraging times we had as a team, but how in the end we triumphed. I had Doug bring out the trophy, while I explained that they could be proud that this was every bit their trophy. The team did it together. It was easily my best speech ever and I was awarded with loud cheers and applause.

It was time for the refreshments and all the wrestlers were elbowing for a place in the serving line. I was standing, waiting for things to be served, when Eugene came up to me.

"Good speech, Coach."

"Thanks, Eugene," I said. "What did you particularly like about it?"

"Well, you said something about the trophy, but I can't remember much else. The best part was when it ended 'cause now it's time to eat." And Eugene stepped into the serving line.

I should have known that after the season is over, the only thing that is important to a wrestler is: when is it time to eat?